# Teaching Strategies for the College Classroom

Most books about college teaching contain exhortations to improve teaching, but they don't tell *how*. This is a different book because it

- describes in detail four theories about how people learn

- develops each theory into a teaching strategy that can be employed by any college teacher

- gives examples which illustrate how each strategy can be applied in a classroom setting.

**Teaching Strategies for the College Classroom** is a book written for individual professors in all fields of study who want to improve their teaching. It is also useful as a text for

- faculty development workshops

- new faculty institutes

- graduate teaching assistant seminars

- courses on college teaching.

**James R. Davis** is Associate Professor of Higher Education and Associate Vice Chancellor for Academic Affairs at the University of Denver.

# James R. Davis

# Teaching Strategies for the College Classroom

**WESTVIEW SPECIAL STUDIES IN HIGHER EDUCATION**

# Westview Press

Copyright 1976 by Westview Press, Inc.

Published 1976 in the United States of America by

Westview Press, Inc.
1898 Flatiron Court
Boulder, Colorado 80301
Frederick A. Praeger, Publisher & Editorial Director

Library of Congress Cataloging in Publication Data

Davis, James R.    1936–
    Teaching strategies for the college classroom.

    Bibliography:  p.
    1. College teaching.  2. Lecture method in
    teaching.
I.  Title
LB2331.D38      378.1'7           76–1905
ISBN 0–89158–033–6 (cl.) ISBN 0–89158–104–9 (ppr.)

Printed in the United States of America

# *Preface*

"Another book on college teaching?" you may ask. "Surely too many have been written already!"

It is true that there are many books about college teaching. Oddly enough, only a few of them provide help for the college professor who wants to be more effective in the classroom. The books which claim to be about college teaching cover a wide range of topics. Many include sections which recount the history of higher education. Others are expositions of a particular philosophy of education. Some contain practical lists of do's and don't's. Still others recount the characteristics of "effective" teachers. Some tell how to evaluate teachers. Others explore instructional problems in a particular discipline. (For an extensive review of the books on college teaching see the bibliographic essay beginning on page 113.) But few of these books speak directly about the teacher's task, the way students learn, and the teaching strategies that are appropriate for the college classroom. The important variables in the teaching-learning situation are often passed over or treated superficially; and the professor finds, with some disappointment, that most of the books about teaching aren't very helpful. Hopefully, this is a different book on college teaching, because it explores in depth some viable teaching strategies for the college classroom.

Most college teachers, given reasonable time for discussion, can agree upon goals. It is generally agreed that our work with students involves more than their training, though some training may take place. Likewise our task goes beyond teaching students a subject, although giving students a thorough grasp of the content of a discipline or field of study is at the heart of what we hope to achieve. Most college teachers are aiming at something higher, some ideal form of the liberally educated person, a civilized being with more than the well-stocked mind. Such a person has acquired a habit of reflection and inquiry, a scholarly approach to social issues, a concern for human values, an aesthetic sense and an insatiable desire for meaning. The educated person we hope to produce is reasonable, open to new evidence, slow to judge, and able to make distinctions and note exceptions. It sounds like catalogue rhetoric, true; but most professors would agree, perhaps with minor qualifications, that the goal of instruction is clear: to produce educated persons.

But what is not clear is *how?* What is the process by which we nurture educated persons? What means best suit this end? What strategies will achieve such a noble ideal? About such matters there is much dispute.

The major assumptions of this book are that professors representing diverse fields of study share a common goal as teachers, that this goal—the nurture of educated persons—has been adequately conceived, and that our greatest deficit as teachers has to do not with goals but with the *process* of education. Although our goals may vary somewhat from field to field and institution to institution, there is an underlying mission we accept and share. The central question is: How can we achieve what we set out to achieve?

There is renewed interest in college teaching today. Many colleges and universities have instituted faculty development programs focused on teaching improvement. A major federal program, The Fund for the Improvement of

Postsecondary Education, makes funding available for the improvement of instruction. Some graduate schools are taking more seriously the task of preparing their graduate assistants as teachers. And out there in the classrooms, on the other side of the lectern, students who have grown accustomed to better teaching in their preparatory education are simply demanding better teaching. More positively, college professors have grown genuinely interested in teaching. They talk about it more and reflect on the bewildering array of instructional options open to them. They have come to realize that effective teaching involves both process and content, and they are as apt to be found reading books on operant learning theory and small group processes as books in their academic discipline.

All of this is occurring at a time when the available knowledge about the teaching-learning process is expanding and finding its way into the hands of professors. There are some who would still argue, of course, that we know nothing about teaching and even less about how people learn. A graduate student chided me recently as we passed four rows of empty stacks in a section of our new library: "This is where we keep our accumulated wisdom on the teaching-learning process." But the plea of ignorance, once a convenient rationalization, is increasingly a display of ignorance. We do "know" some things about how people learn, and the things we know have clear implications for teaching. There is surely no consensus about what we know and, consequently, no lack of argument about which particular theory of learning is best. But we have begun to learn certain things about how behavior is affected by reinforcement, how people process and remember information, how question-asking behavior is related to learning, and how people learn through active involvement in small groups. There *are* teaching strategies that a college teacher can learn to employ effectively in the classroom.

This book has grown out of a course on college teaching offered regularly at the University of Denver. The four teaching strategies, which make up the core of the book, have been presented in workshop format during the summer, as training institutes for graduate teaching assistants, and as sections of faculty development workshops held at several colleges around the country. The content of these chapters has been developed over a period of five years in conversation with college teachers and colleagues from every region of the country and every type of institution. Thus the strategies presented here have been discussed and criticized extensively by a wide variety of college teachers who have reflected seriously on the task of teaching.

During the summers of 1972 and 1973 a Workshop on College Teaching was co-sponsored by the University of Denver School of Education and the North Central Association of Colleges and Secondary Schools. Through special funds made available by the North Central Association, several guests were invited to be on campus, to prepare papers, and to make presentations. The content of the workshops, and subsequently of this book, has been immeasurably increased through my association with those colleagues. In particular, I wish to acknowledge my indebtedness to the work of the following:

Dr. Alton Barbour; Associate Professor of Speech Communication; University of Denver; Denver, Colorado

Dr. James Block; Assistant Professor of Education; University of California at Santa Barbara; Santa Barbara, California

Dr. Ruth Day; Associate Professor of Psychology; Yale University; New Haven, Connecticut

Dr. Alvin Goldberg; Professor of Speech Communication; University of Denver; Denver, Colorado

Dr. John Hollenbach; Professor of English; Hope College; Holland, Michigan

Dr. Robert Karsten, Vice-President for Administration; Gustavus Adolphus College; St. Peter, Minnesota

Dr. Joel Macht; Associate Professor of Educational Psychology; University of Denver; Denver, Colorado

Dr. Ohmer Milton; Professor of Psychology and Director, Learning Research Center, University of Tennessee; Knoxville, Tennessee

Dr. Allan O. Pfnister; Professor of Higher Education; University of Denver; Denver, Colorado

Dr. Bradley Sagen; Associate Professor of Higher Education; The University of Iowa; Iowa City, Iowa

Dr. Charles Weingartner; Professor of Education; University of South Florida; Tampa, Florida

In many places I have drawn directly upon their ideas and insights.

The book opens with a discussion of the "conventional wisdom" about teaching and a review of the research on college teaching. In the next four chapters the four teaching strategies are presented and elaborated. Each strategy grows out of a particular theory about how people learn and contains implications for what teachers do in the college classroom. The final chapter provides some guidance on choosing a teaching strategy, and the bibliographic essay contains an extended discussion of the books on college teaching. The format for this book provides space in the margin for notes, and it is hoped that the reader will "interact" with the content of the text by jotting down reactions and ideas.

I especially want to thank my wife, Nancilee, for her criticism of the manuscript and help in proofreading, Margaret Wick for aiding in the bibliographic research, A&D Copy & Typing Service for typing the manuscript, Lynne Rienner for editing the copy, and Fred Praeger for his editorial assistance and encouragement.

March 1976                                         James R. Davis
Denver, Colorado

# Contents

# What Is Known, What Is Said

There is a lot of cheap talk about college teaching.
Everyone has an opinion, probably because everyone at
some point has experienced very "good" and very "bad"
teaching.

It is a favorite pastime of students to discuss their
professors; and it is instructive, if you ever get the
chance, to listen. Much of the discussion is personal.
They don't like someone's ugly ties or oxford shoes.
So and so twitches and blinks. Prof. X puts you to
sleep and Prof. Y shouts too much. Dr. Jones is never
prepared. Dr. Smith never allows time for questions
and Ms. Barker always gets off the subject. The philosophers
always answer your questions with questions, the English
profs expect too much, and the chem. profs always smell
bad. Nobody takes a personal interest. But the very
worst is the guy who puts you down for asking a dumb
question. That's inexcusable.

So it goes .... a lot of glib opinions without much
depth. But then, why should we expect more? Sitting
in classrooms for 12 to 16 years—especially classrooms
where the teaching has been less than outstanding—
hardly qualifies one to be an expert on teaching. Should
we really expect students to have reflected deeply on
what the teaching-learning process is all about? We
should attend to their comments (e.g., it *isn't,* in fact,

productive to "put people down"), but we can hardly anticipate that our students will come up with full-blown theories about effective teaching.

The talk in the faculty lounge isn't much better. Most faculty members want smaller classes, lighter teaching loads, and fewer committee assignments. "If we just had these . . . and better students! We must do something about admission standards. The students here just aren't motivated. They can't read; they can't write; they can't *think*." There is a pause in the discussion. A neophyte instructor suggests that the students could be reached if they had better instruction. A brief discussion follows but is ended abruptly when the most senior member of the geriatric oligarchy pontificates, "It's always been my opinion that great teachers are born not made." A conversation-stopper, indeed!

But most college teachers grow dissatisfied with the glib talk about teaching. We know in our hearts, or at least we suspect, that teaching is a much more complicated task than it appears on the surface, and we begin to search for a more solid basis for our opinions. Being academically inclined, i.e., scientific, we feel a need to look at the evidence. Sooner or later the questions arise: What do we know about college teaching? Are there research studies? What do the studies show?

## Research on College Teaching

There are, indeed, research studies; it seems sometimes that there is no end to them. The following sampling of journal article titles illustrates the nature and scope of these studies:

> "The Effects of a Programmed Textbook on Achievement Under Three Techniques of Instruction"

"The Effect of Intelligence and Social Atmosphere on Group Problem Solving Behavior"

"The Effect of Class Size on Achievement and Attitudes"

"An Experimental Study of the Use of Lectures to Large Groups of Students in Teaching the Fundamentals of Speech"

"The Relative Merits of Lecture and Recitation in Teaching College Physics"

"A Comparison Between Lecture and Conference Methods of Teaching Psychology"

"Reading Improvement as a Function of Student Personality and Teaching Method"

"Comparison of Directed Self-study Versus Lecture in Teaching General Psychology"

What do the studies conclude? That is a difficult question. Some studies make significant conclusions about a particular teaching method, but one does not need to search far for other, seemingly similar, studies which contradict those conclusions. Unfortunately, most of the studies produce the researcher's anathema: "No significant differences." It is important, therefore, to examine a collection of studies, not simply individual studies, to see if there are any overall trends in this growing body of research literature. Fortunately, such reviews have been completed by some very competent scholars.

One of these reviews was done by Wilbert McKeachie for a chapter in the first volume of a reference work entitled *Handbook of Research on Teaching*, edited by N. L. Gage (McKeachie, 1963). While the *Handbook* includes chapters which review many aspects of teaching at all levels, McKeachie's chapter focuses on studies of teaching at the college and university level. McKeachie reviews studies which examine lecturing, discussion, laboratory methods, independent study, and automated teaching methods. He finds the usual contradictions and studies with "no significant differences," but he formulates some tentative conclusions. Lecturing seems to be an effective way of communicating information, but other methods seem to be more important in achieving higher cognitive and attitudinal objectives. Discussions prove helpful in achieving certain objectives, but vary in their effectiveness according to the manner in which the discussion is conducted, the size of the group, and the degree of "student-centeredness." Laboratory methods develop problem-solving abilities, provided that the emphasis in the laboratory is on solving problems. While independent study seems to increase motivation, it may be less effective in bringing about other desirable educational outcomes. Automated techniques vary in their effectiveness according to the quality of the materials used and the objectives pursued.

McKeachie's earlier survey has been brought up to date with a more recent review published as an ERIC Clearinghouse Report (McKeachie, 1970). In that report McKeachie is much more cognizant of the methodological problems involved in doing research on college teaching, but he still finds in the studies he reviews certain trends and tendencies. He concludes that small classes seem to be better for basic retention, problem solving, and attitude differentiation. Discussion method seems best for increasing problem-solving ability and for dealing with attitudes and motivation. Large lectures coupled with small discussion sections seem to be generally more effective than lecture sections of unwieldy size. Student-centered discussions seem more favorable for the more complex educational outcomes. Students may not learn more with automated devices, but they may learn more efficiently or like it better. Although McKeachie makes no direct attack on the methodology of the studies he reviews, he is cautious in drawing conclusions. The overall theme is that different methods seem to be effective for different objectives.

A more recent collection of research can be found in Ohmer Milton's *Alternatives to the Traditional* (1972). Milton makes the case that the effectiveness of traditional methods of instruction at the college level has never been proven. Traditional methods are vigorously

4

supported, yet there seems to be little concrete evidence to warrant such enthusiasm for conventional teaching and learning arrangements. In developing his argument, Milton discusses a wide variety of studies done on different aspects of college teaching. He notes, for example, that the tremendous assumption about transfer of training, which underlies much of the teaching that takes place at the college level, has been generally disproven; that there is little evidence that the four-year lockstep is the only, or necessarily best, format for a college education; and that there is some evidence that students do not require nearly the surveillance in the learning process that their professors think they need. Milton cites studies that cast doubt on the traditional grading and evaluation systems employed at the college level, studies that suggest that grades are unrelated to job performance and that most tests penalize bright students. The studies Milton has drawn together demonstrate that the current research on college teaching fails to lend much support for continuing to use traditional teaching methods. Unfortunately, there is not much evidence that alternative methods are much better. Milton admits the lack of evidence, but concludes by asking, "What do I have to lose?"

The American Educational Research Association recently has published a *Second Handbook of Research on Teaching,* an expanded and up-to-date version of the earlier volume edited by Gage. It contains a current summary of research on teaching in higher education, in particular, a summary of research on "Teaching Technology and Methods" (Cohen, Rose, and Trent, 1973) in which it is reported that students experience higher tension, poorer achievement, and less satisfaction in competitive as opposed to cooperative class discussions. One study demonstrates a high interaction among instructional methods, learner characteristics, and subject matters in a pattern that may be designated "learning style." Another study suggests that students with high creativity and high social needs perform best in small discussion groups. Several studies of class size were inconclusive. One noted that large group lectures combined with small group discussion were no more or less effective than conventional classes of 50 or 60 students.

The conclusions of another review are much more systematic but also much more pessimistic. In 1968 a controversial monograph was published entitled *The Teaching-Learning Paradox: A Comparative Analysis of College Teaching Methods* (Dubin and Taveggia, 1968). Its authors undertook a systematic analysis of the research on college teaching. Their analysis involved some complicated procedures, but in essence they set about to tally the results of the studies on a balance sheet. They analyzed the studies which showed no significant differences, but they also balanced those studies favoring one method with those favoring another. The end result was that one trend cancelled out another. Their conclusions are summarized in the following statements: "In the foregoing paragraphs we have reported the results of a reanalysis of the data from 91 comparative studies of college teaching technologies conducted between 1924 and 1965. These data demonstrate clearly and unequivocally that there is no measurable difference among truly distinctive teaching methods of college instruction when evaluated by student performance on final examinations" (p. 35).

## Does Anything Make Any Difference?

What are we to conclude? If there seem to be no differences between teaching methods, does anything make any difference? Is one method as good as any other? Is there any reason to hold workshops on teaching or to institute faculty-development programs? Should this endless discussion of teaching methods cease? Is one teacher's opinion as good as another's in the faculty lounge discussions? Even worse, are teachers perhaps born and not made?

It is tempting to conclude, when faced with an unresolved

problem, that there are no answers and that what one does makes no difference, since there is no factual basis for a decision. It may be, however, that the answer remains elusive not because there is no answer, but because the problem is more complex than was anticipated. Perhaps the answer remains obscured because the question has been put in the wrong way. Perhaps the methodology is insufficient for analyzing the complexity of the phenomena.

It was exactly that conclusion which Dubin and Taveggia drew from their studies. They were astounded to find that competent scholars would persist in repeating studies using methods which had already yielded inconclusive results. The need is not for replication, they argued, but for a new research design. Several pages of their monograph are devoted to an attack on the conventional design for undertaking research on college teaching.

## A New Research Design

Most research on college teaching follows a rather simple design. Teaching Method A, let us say, using the lecture method, is compared with Teaching Method B, using the discussion method. Student performance on final or standardized exams is used to measure and compare the teaching effectiveness of Teaching Method A and Teaching Method B. As even the neophyte can guess, there is something wrong with that design. Teaching is more complicated than that. There seems to be a far greater range of variables which enter into the teaching-learning process than are represented by the labels "lecture" and "discussion" method. What about the materials used? What about the objectives? What about the teaching strategy? And what about the students themselves? Will they all respond in the same way? Will the learning outcomes for one student be different from those of another? Will the student evaluate his learning by standards which might be quite different from those used by the teacher?

While Dubin and Taveggia were attacking the conventional model for doing research on college teaching, another set of scholars was engaged in a systematic analysis of the problem and the development of a new model. In a provocative but almost unnoticed journal article, Laurence and Lila Siegel set forth guidelines which are sending inquiries about the effectiveness of college teaching techniques in a new direction (Siegel and Siegel, 1967). Siegel and Siegel point out that comparisons between two or more instructional procedures can be made only if the procedures are independent and homogeneous. By independent, they mean that the procedure (lecturing, for example) must be sufficiently isolated from other factors to be considered a distinct and separate influence on the process. Lecturing must be sufficiently differentiated from providing information through a textbook to be regarded as a separate and distinct entity. If what takes place in a lecture is not sufficiently different from what takes place when a student reads a text, it is not surprising that those students in the control section (Method B—discussion), who also read the text, do as well on the final exam as those who hear lectures. Before one can make comparisons between teaching methods, one must first be sure that the methods are distinct and different.

The procedures must also be homogeneous. By this the authors mean that the method must involve only one variable. The method to be examined cannot be a general method which is in fact several methods subsumed under one label. Behind the generic label "discussion method," one must make inquiries into the nature of the verbal interaction taking place, the role and personality of the teacher, the objectives of the discussion, the nature of the inquiry process, the atmosphere of acceptance, and other factors. "Discussion method," therefore, is probably not a homogeneous procedure; it is a collection of variables, not a single variable. In comparing teaching procedures, one must isolate single variables for comparison.

Furthermore, the authors contend, final examinations are probably inadequate criterion measures. Student performance on final exams (the dependent variable in conventional research designs) can be motivated by factors which range far beyond the classroom methodology and may include such familiar influences as another student's carefully taken lecture notes or the desire to avoid the aversive stimulus of catching the devil from home. Most final exams test a narrow range of cognitive skills and probably are not adequate measures of teaching effectiveness.

What is needed, the authors argue, is a multivariate research paradigm which is sufficiently broad to include the full multiplicity and patterning of factors entering the teaching-learning configuration. Siegel and Siegel suggest that further research on college teaching ought to include an examination of independent and homogeneous variables in the following categories: learning environments, instructor variables, learner variables, and course variables. The criteria ought to include a full range of learning outcomes and achievements. The research design probably should employ the statistical techniques of factor analysis and multivariate analysis.

What structure would emerge from such a design? What results could be anticipated? One might identify certain key variables to examine and manipulate, holding constant, to the extent that it is possible, all other variables. Thus, one might vary and examine class size, attendance requirements, personal contact between teacher and student, students' previous knowledge of the subject and general academic aptitude, and teaching strategies. One teaching strategy might involve discussion using an inquiry approach, and the other might involve a lecture with a daily end-of-period test and immediate feedback of results. The criterion measures might test for ability to retain information, to solve problems, and to state a position. In other words, one would select what seem to be the most important learning environment variables, instructor variables, learner variables, and course variables and gather data on each of them.

The results of such research might reveal, for example, that students who had high academic aptitude and some previous knowledge of the subject were best at factual recall if taught in large classes with minimal contact with the instructor under a lecture teaching strategy involving sophisticated awareness of information processing techniques. In other words, certain variables would tend to interact with other variables and would tend to suggest a pattern of instruction which will produce certain results for certain kinds of students. The underlying research question for such a model might be phrased as follows: Under what conditions do what kinds of students learn what things?

## Everything Matters

Most readers of this volume probably will not engage in systematic research on college teaching. The statistical methods are available, the theory is in hand, and the need for such studies is great. It is more likely, however, that the typical college teacher will need to attend to more immediate and pressing practical concerns. Thinking through the problems involved in doing research on college teaching is a helpful exercise, however, for defining what is at stake in the teaching-learning process. For the classroom teacher, the practical question is more likely to be phrased: What do I need to pay attention to if I am to become a more effective college teacher? What are the important variables over which I might have some control? In other words: Does anything make any difference? Contrary to the original inclination to

10

respond by saying "Nothing matters," it seems more likely now that the answer will be, "Yes, everything matters!"

Everything matters! The class size may make a difference. The entering behavior and motivation of the students may matter. The intellectual climate and even the geography of the institution may matter. The nature and pacing of rewards for learning may matter. The way information is received, processed, and remembered may matter. The process by which inquiry is carried on may matter. The quality of interpersonal relationships between teacher and student may matter. The ways students are examined and evaluated may matter. Different students will probably respond to instruction in different ways. And the learning outcomes for some will be different from the achievements of others. Everything matters.

Furthermore, most of the variables are related in important ways to other variables; no variable functions in simple isolation from the rest. The ecologist's model serves as a helpful way of understanding the teaching environment. Everything matters and every important factor in the process is related to all the other factors. Our tendency in thinking about teaching, as in thinking about the environment, is to reduce complex interactions to simple cause-effect relationships, to examine the properties of isolated parts of the process at the expense of developing a comprehensive overview of the total system. If we are to improve our teaching we must examine the total ecological web of the learning environment.

But it is rather overwhelming, even frightening, to know that everything matters, especially when we know that as college teachers we can't control all the variables. This is often why the most dedicated efforts to effect learning sometimes end in great frustration. But if we cannot control all the variables—and we need to come to terms with that fact—we can at least control some of the variables. We can control to a large extent one of the key variables: teaching behavior. We can reflect deeply upon our role as teachers in the teaching-learning process and devise teaching strategies which are based on theory, are consistent, and are carried out with single-minded dedication.

## Teaching Strategy: A Definition

The *Random House Dictionary of the English Language* defines strategy as "a plan, method, or series of maneuvers or strategems for obtaining a specific goal or result." Applied to college teaching, the term strategy refers to a plan, method, or series of activities designed to achieve a particular educational goal. Sound teaching strategies are based upon clear understandings of how people learn. Different strategies involve differing conceptions of what learning is and how it takes place. The debate about such issues is not easily resolved, nor should it be. The important point, for our purposes, is that the effective college teacher must employ *some* strategy.

This is precisely the point at which most talk about college teaching falters, whether the superficial criticism of students, the aimless discussions in the faculty lounge, or the sophisticated-sounding reports of research on college teaching. Almost none of the talk about teaching gets down to examining whether or not the teacher has a strategy for achieving goals.

Most teaching at the college level has followed a convention known as the "talking tradition." For some reason it is assumed that a college professor, well prepared in a discipline, can walk into a classroom, start talking, and as day follows night, something educational will just happen. It is the thesis of this book that effective teaching doesn't just happen; to the contrary, effective teaching depends in large part upon the instructor's having a clear set of goals and a sufficient strategy for reaching those goals. My hunch is that most professors can greatly improve their teaching by persistently applying one or more of the teaching strategies described in the chapters which follow.

## References

Cohen, Arthur, Clare Rose, and James W. Trent. "Teaching Technology and Methods." In Robert M. W. Travers, ed., *Second Handbook of Research on Teaching,* pp. 1023-1035. Chicago: Rand McNally Co., 1973.

Dubin, Robert, and Thomas G. Taveggia. *The Teaching-Learning Paradox: A Comparative Analysis of College Teaching Methods.* Eugene, Ore.: Center for the Advanced Study of Educational Administration, 1968.

McKeachie, Wilbert J. "Research on College Teaching: A Review." Report 6, ERIC Clearinghouse on Higher Education, Washington, 1970.

McKeachie, Wilbert J. "Research on Teaching at the College and University Level." In N. L. Gage, ed., *Handbook of Research on Teaching,* pp. 1118-1172. Chicago: Rand McNally Co., 1963.

Milton, Ohmer. *Alternatives to the Traditional.* San Francisco: Jossey-Bass, 1972.

Siegel, Laurence, and Lila C. Siegel. "A Multivariate Paradigm for Educational Research." *Psychological Bulletin,* 68(1967): 306-326.

# STRATEGY 1:
# Employing
# Instructional Systems

It has been said, "An educated man knows what he is doing." That simple statement implies that an educated person not only does the "right things" but that he or she knows why those things are being done. Options have been considered, plans have been laid, and a conscious choice has been made. Unfortunately, too many college teachers don't know (in this sense) what they are doing, i.e., their activity in the classroom is governed by convention rather than conscious choice.

In recent years some college teachers, as a matter of conscious choice, have begun to develop a more analytic and systematic approach to teaching. They have begun to specify instructional goals more clearly, they have developed stepwise progressions to achieve these goals, and they have begun to employ with conscious intent various kinds of incentives. Some have utilized programmed instruction and computer-assisted instruction. Others have developed entire self-paced courses. Some have created electronic feedback systems, while still others have experimented with new types of criterion-referenced grading systems. Such "instructional systems" may be formal or informal, they may employ highly sophisticated equipment or they may involve crude attempts just to be more organized. Most of the concepts used in these various kinds of instructional systems grow out of principles developed by behavioral psychologists. It is helpful, therefore, to know something about their work.

## Behavioral Learning Theory

The name of B. F. Skinner is now a household word. His name is identified with that branch of psychology which has come to be known as behaviorism. Skinner is today the world's most articulate behaviorist, and his theories have been popularized, so that most college teachers are familiar with at least some of his ideas. But Skinner's work is the culmination of a long tradition; his investigations are based upon the previous work of Fechner, Wundt, Guthrie, Thorndike, and Watson.

It was Watson who said that "the subject matter of human psychology is the behavior of the human being" (Watson, 1924, p. 2). Behaviorists are not interested in the mind, the emotions, and various states of consciousness. They are interested in behavior. Although much of their experimental work has involved rats, pigeons, and cats, their primary interest, as Watson notes, is *human* behavior.

The basic principles of behavioral learning theory are relatively easy to grasp. The first principle is that behavior is affected by its consequences. In Skinner's own words: "Behavior is said to be *strengthened* by its consequences, and for that reason, the consequences are called *'reinforcers.'* Thus, when a hungry organism exhibits behavior that produces food, the behavior is reinforced by that consequence and is therefore more likely to recur" (Skinner, 1974, p. 39).

The most common model for "operant" or instrumental conditioning is:

$$R \longrightarrow S$$

R is the response. It is followed by a reinforcing stimulus, S. It is what occurs immediately after behavior that counts, i.e., that influences the likelihood that such behavior

16

will be repeated. This basic principle has become known as Thorndike's Law of Effect (Keller, 1954).

## Reinforcement

There are two basic types of reinforcers, positive stimuli and aversive (punishing) stimuli. A positive reinforcer, in Skinner's words, "strengthens any behavior that produces it: a glass of water is positively reinforcing when we are thirsty, and if we then draw and drink a glass of water, we are more likely to do so on similar occasions" (Skinner, 1974, p. 46). Behaviors that precede these consequences, therefore, are likely to be repeated. Positive reinforcers can be anything that an individual is willing to put forth effort to obtain.

Aversive or punishing stimuli, on the other hand, are those things that an individual is willing to work hard to avoid. Behaviors that precede these consequences are likely not to be repeated. Note that the definition of a reinforcer depends not on the properties of the reinforcer itself, but on how the individual responds to it. Food is not reinforcing on a full stomach. Not every stimulus is equally reinforcing for all individuals. Some students will work hard for grades; others find them inconsequential.

## Procedures for Increasing or Decreasing the Frequency of Behavior

There are two procedures employed for initiating, maintaining, or increasing the frequency of behavior: positive reinforcement and negative reinforcement. (Negative reinforcement is often confused with punishment, but their differences will be apparent below.) Positive reinforcement simply involves rewarding behavior with something that someone will work for. In the college classroom typical reinforcers include attention, recognition, praise, confirmation of correct answers, free time or a day off, time for social interaction, points, grades, Dean's lists, and other awards and forms of approbation. Perhaps the best reinforcement comes through the task itself when the student gets things right and finds things out. Positive reinforcement often seems to take on the form of a bribe or incentive ("If you'll do this, then . . ."), and in that form is operating according to what is known as Premack's Principle, or more affectionately, Grandma's Rule.

Negative reinforcement involves removing an aversive stimulus, something an individual will work hard to avoid. The emphasis is on avoidance or removal, thus a negative reinforcer often turns out to be a threat. Most college students will work hard to avoid low grades, suspension lists, critical remarks, or the embarrassment that accompanies being ill-prepared. Although the stimulus is aversive, the possibility of its removal *increases* the frequency of desired behaviors. Much "studying behavior" is initiated, increased, or maintained by negative reinforcement.

There are also two procedures for decreasing the frequency of behavior: extinction and punishment. The process of withholding reinforcement is known as extinction. The concept is adequately summarized in the phrase, "Leave it alone and it will go away." When a teacher withholds attention from a student who "overparticipates" in a discussion (and when all other sources of reinforcement are also withheld), the student's participation will probably decrease. If a shy student is given no reinforcement for participation, that participation will probably "extinguish" or cease altogether unless the teacher recognizes the need for a little reinforcement (Macht, 1975b).

Punishment is the direct application of an aversive stimulus. Most of us need no further definition of punishment; we've experienced it. Fortunately most corporal punishment has been eliminated from collegiate education—if for no other reason than the imposing physical size of each succeeding student generation makes it dangerous— but as Skinner has pointed out, "ridicule . . . sarcasm, criticism, incarceration, extra school or home work, the withdrawal of privileges, forced labor, ostracism, being put on silence and fines" are still used and permit the teacher "to spare the rod without spoiling the child" (Skinner, 1968, p. 96).

Punishment, however, has definite problems associated with its use. For one thing, it is possible to stop or eliminate certain behaviors with punishment, but it is almost impossible to teach correct responses. English teachers, for example, who return themes bloodied with corrections, but with little reinforcement of *correct* responses, will probably never teach their students to write correctly. Furthermore, punishment has certain associative or generalization effects. A student who is "put down" continually by a professor soon learns to dislike not only the professor, but the subject and the college as well. The behavior that is punished will decrease, but so will other associated behaviors, like coming to class. Punishment also has emotional side effects. In pigeons an electric shock causes some strange wing-flapping and body-pecking. In students the emotional responses to punishment may include fear, anger, frustration, anxiety, or even illness. Finally, punishment often results in counter-aggression. If a professor consistently employs punishment, the day will soon come when students will strike back (Macht, 1975a).

## Shaping

The procedures for increasing or decreasing the frequency of certain behaviors "work," and they work automatically, i.e., whether the teacher is aware of them or not. Students stop coming to class when a teacher is sarcastic, whether the teacher knows he is sarcastic or not. The question is not whether or not the principles "work"; the question is: How can reinforcement be employed consciously and effectively by the classroom teacher?

Let us return to the laboratory for a moment to consider how an animal is "taught" a specific task. Suppose that a psychologist wishes to train a pigeon to turn a complete circle in a clockwise direction. The first thing the trainer must do is to prescribe the goal clearly in "behavioral" terms so that everyone can agree upon whether or not the pigeon is performing the desired behavior. The next thing to do is to put the pigeon in the "Skinner-box" or some other laboratory setting to see if the pigeon is already able to turn clockwise circles. We call this "taking the pigeon's baserate." Let's assume that the pigeon can't turn circles; and that like most pigeons it just goes walking about, cooing and poking its beak into every nook and cranny of the box. How would you get it to turn clockwise circles? The answer is to break the task into a series of steps, successive approximations of the goal. Thus, when the pigeon makes the very first move—it may simply shift its weight to the right foot—it is reinforced with a food pellet. Next the pigeon steps to the right and leans to the right. Another food pellet appears. Next the pigeon takes two steps to the right and twists its neck back and to the right. A reinforcer appears. The process continues through the series of successive approximations until the goal (a clockwise circle) is attained (Skinner, 1953).

The same shaping procedure is utilized for various forms of instruction involving humans. The procedures are simple.

1. A clear behavioral goal must be identified.

2. A baserate measure of existing skill or present performance level must be taken.

3. The task must be broken into steps.

4. Successive approximations of the goal are reinforced until the goal is reached.

The model can be diagrammed quite simply as follows (Macht, 1975a, p. 177):

Teacher's Goal

10
9
8
7
6    Small steps (approximations)
5
4
Reinforcements  3
2
1

Student's Present Performance Level

All instructional systems, whether simple or highly complex, rely on this basic model which grows out of behavioral learning theory. Let's look at some of the applications that educators have made of the basic model.

## Implications for Teaching

Behavioral learning theory can be applied in the college classroom in a variety of ways. Obviously, teachers can guide the course of a discussion by the way reinforcement is handled. The general atmosphere of a class can be established as reinforcing or punishing. Student motivation can be increased by more frequent use of a variety of incentives. Such applications of behavioral learning theory are directed toward the immediate behavior patterns of teachers and students and fall in the category of "behavior modification techniques." A more sustained application of behavioral learning theory results in complex instructional systems. We shall examine some of them in detail.

## Behavioral Objectives

What was once a small cult has grown into a significant movement, namely, that trend among educators to specify learning outcomes in the form of behavioral objectives. Educators usually make a distinction between goals and behavioral objectives (Davis, Alexander, and Yelon, 1974). Goals are expressed in broad and often abstract terms. College teachers often say they want their students to "appreciate" music or "understand" history or "really understand" economics. (The number of "really's" preceding the verb really doesn't matter.) The problem with vague goals is that no one—neither the teacher nor the student—can be sure when the goals have been reached. To arrive at some consensus about the attainment of goals, we need to utilize objectives that include some statements about measurable behaviors.

College teachers often resist stating their goals in the form of behavioral objectives. Ralph Tyler has described the issue this way:

> One common question is "Why is it now considered important to define objectives clearly, when teachers in the past have done excellent work without having a clear statement of goals?" It is certainly true that many teachers have a sense of what is important for students to learn and some of them are able to translate this notion of educational goals into relevant learning

experiences for the student without ever having put down on paper what these implicit aims are. However, many others have not carried their thinking beyond the point of selecting the content to be presented. They have not considered carefully what students are to do with the content. . . . For example, in several college history courses the teachers told me that their objectives were to develop understanding on the part of students of the way in which past events, episodes, and the like influenced later conditions and problems. They also said that they wanted the students to learn to draw on various sources of information about the past and to be able to explain what is happening today partly in terms of this influence of the past. But in spite of mentioning these kinds of objectives, the teachers' performance in class consisted primarily in lecturing on what they had learned about the historical period under study and quizzing students on the lecture and related reading. The result was that the student, watching the performance of the teacher, thought that what was expected of him was to be able to do the same thing. He felt that he should memorize what people knew about this period rather than develop any of the desired abilities and skills [Lindvall, 1964, p. 77].

The more global goals that college teachers hope to achieve can be reached best if the goals are further specified in behavioral terms. Behavioral objectives "are relatively specific statements of learning outcomes expressed from the learner's point-of-view and telling what the learner is to *do* at the end of the instruction" (Burns, 1972, p. 5). They cite specific behaviors that can be observed. The words used in behavioral objectives must be specific. Robert Mager (1962, p. 11) has constructed an exemplary list of vague and specific infinitives:

| Words Open to Many Interpretations | Words Open to Fewer Interpretations |
|---|---|
| to know | to write |
| to understand | to recite |
| to *really* understand | to identify |
| to appreciate | to differentiate |
| to *fully* appreciate | to solve |
| to grasp the significance of | to construct |
| to enjoy | to list |
| to believe | to compare |
| to have faith in | to contrast |

Many such lists of "specific" verbs have been developed by educators interested in writing behavioral objectives.* One list notes 24 terms for higher-order specifications of the infinitive "to understand" (Burns, 1972, p. 102). The point is clear: A well-expressed behavioral objective uses very specific language.

The classic specifications for behavioral objectives were developed by Robert Mager. He suggests that a well-written behavioral objective contains a statement of *terminal behavior,* what the learner will be doing when he is demonstrating that he has achieved the objective; a statement of *conditions* under which the behavior will be expected to occur; and a statement of *criteria,* the standards of acceptable performance (Mager, 1962). A typical behavioral objective for a college class follows:

> Given a one-term course in music appreciation, the student, on a paper and pencil test, will be able to listen to and identify 25 out of 30 excerpts of compositions selected at random from the 50 works studied. Identification must be by composer's last name, artistic period (Renaissance, Baroque, Classical, etc.) and general music form (symphony, overture, trio, quintet, etc.).

*The best known of the various statements of educational outcomes is the three-volume *Taxonomy of Educational Objectives:* Handbook I, *Cognitive Domain,* Benjamin S. Bloom, ed.; Handbook II, *Affective Domain,* D. R. Krathwohl, Benjamin S. Bloom, and B. B. Masia, eds.; Handbook III, *Psycho-Motor Domain,* Anita Harrow, ed.

The objective calls for a specific set of terminal behaviors, and it states the conditions under which the task is to be performed and the criteria for acceptable performance. The task is of a fairly high order. It requires that the student know each of the 50 compositions thoroughly and assumes that the student can identify stylistic periods readily and can tell the general form of the composition. The teacher who uses such an objective is in a much better position to evaluate a student's performance (and his own teaching performance) than is the teacher who simply operates with some vague notion about wanting students to "know" the music studied in the course.

The case for behavioral objectives is hard to refute. Think back to the pigeon. A psychologist would never get a pigeon to turn clockwise circles if the psychologist wasn't fairly precise, in the first place, in stating his goals. It just won't work if you ask a pigeon to "really appreciate" circles. The same is true with college students. Although stating objectives in behavioral terms is only the first step in developing a full-blown instructional system, it is a vital step that most college teachers could engage in with great profit.

## Self-Paced Instructional Systems

What are the other components of an instructional system? Once goals have been clearly established, a process for reaching the goals must be developed. In other words, the educational outcomes must be analyzed and the teacher must think through a series of learning experiences (successive approximations) which will enable the student to reach the designated objectives. For example, it is not self-evident how the student mentioned in the behavioral objective cited above is to progress from where he or she is (little or no knowledge of composers, periods, and forms) to the rather complex behavior required in the objective.

Educators have given considerable thought to designing instructional systems. Sometimes a fairly simple concept is obscured and made to appear complex through what seems to be an endless variety of flow diagrams with their attendant boxes, arrows, and feedback loops. Actually the basic principles are very simple, perhaps because they parallel so precisely what happens to the pigeon learning to turn clockwise circles. Figure 1 is a simplification of what you can find in most books on instructional systems (cf. Davis, Alexander, and Yelon, 1974).

The question arises: Has any one at the college level ever employed such instructional systems? The answer is yes. Furthermore, the systems have been designed in such a way to maximize the student's freedom to move through a course at his or her own pace. Perhaps the best known of the pioneering efforts to develop self-paced instructional systems is the psychology course developed by Fred Keller, variously known as PY112 at Arizona State, P-I-P (personalized-individualized-process), or the Keller Plan. The technique was first developed by Keller and his associates in 1966 while establishing a psychology department at the University of Brasília (Milton, 1972).

The course simply involves a very precise set of objectives and a series of learning modules or units designed to help students reach the various objectives. Students are asked to work through the course one unit at a time, progressing at their own pace. Before moving on to the next unit, students are asked to pass a "readiness" test to demonstrate that they can perform the objectives of the present unit. Instruction is provided in a variety of forms—reading, laboratory work, discussions, demonstrations, lectures—and is made available as a majority of the class is ready for it. The course is designed to maximize success and reduce failure and allows some students to finish before the end of the term while others,

26

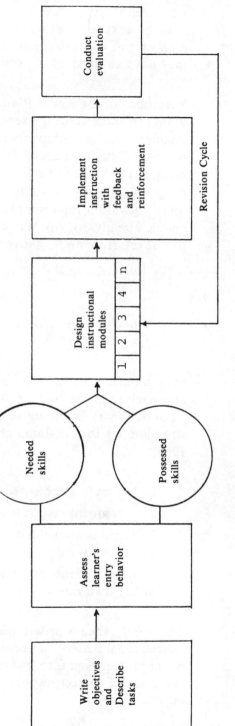

Figure 1

who need the time, are allowed to extend the course into the next term. Students move step by step through each unit of the course and they are done only when they have attained all the objectives.

Variations of the Keller Plan are used on many campuses today. In some cases the technique is called "designed learning" and the behaviors are designated as "competencies," but in most cases the same principles are being applied. Almost all military and industrial training programs use some variation of a systems approach today, based on three simple questions: (a) What can people already do? (b) What do we want them to be able to do? (c) How do we move from a to b?

## Programmed Instruction

Programmed instruction is another variation of the systems approach to instruction although its relation to behavioral learning theory is seldom identified. Programmed instruction has four defining characteristics (Stolurow, 1969):

1. Material is presented in small steps (frames).
2. A frequent response is required of the students.
3. There is immediate confirmation of right and wrong answers.
4. Each student moves through the material at his or her own rate.

Obviously, when a programmer sets about to design instructional materials, behavioral objectives are set, the material is broken into frames, and reinforcement (confirmation of correct responses) is dispensed at proper intervals.

A typical program reads as follows:

Frame 1   Learning occurs when an individual's response is promptly rewarded or _____ .

_____

Reinforced

_____

Frame 2   Reinforcement which consists of presenting sought-after stimuli is called positive reinforcement; reinforcement which consists of terminating unpleasant stimuli (e.g., a loud noise) is called _____ reinforcement.

_____

Negative

_____

Frame 3   Positive and negative reinforcement reward operant behaviors in a process known as _____ conditioning.

_____

Operant

_____

You seem to understand operant conditioning. Turn to page 54. If you want to review the theory further before trying some applications, turn to page 32.

A program can be linear or branching. As in the case of the example above, a branching program will ask the learner to skip ahead or go back and review, depending on the level of performance.

Although a great deal of controversy surrounds the use of programmed learning materials at the college level, there are now some rather sophisticated programmed texts being used in college classrooms. Materials are available in every field and most college teachers will find suitable material in their discipline. An up-to-date notebook on programmed materials in print is available in most libraries.*

## Computer-Assisted Instruction (CAI)

Anything that can be done in a programmed text can also be done with some help from a computer. The special properties of a branching program, in particular, can be greatly enhanced with a computer. Students are presented with frames (either typed on a print-out or projected on a cathode-ray tube) which ask questions or call for a response. When the student responds, the computer "replies" either with a confirmation of the right answer (accompanied by appropriate praise) or with some suggestions about how to get the right answer. A good program will account for all the different responses that a student might make and will "reply" with tailor-made suggestions. Computer-assisted instruction (CAI) is relatively easy to prepare, is fun to work with, and can be incredibly human—after all, humans program the computer.

CAI is now regarded as a supplement to other forms of learning rather than a replacement. Several national conferences have been held on CAI in the undergraduate curriculm,† and the development of programs has now reached a high level of sophistication. Probably the most highly developed CAI available to colleges and universities is that which has been produced cooperatively as Project PLATO through the University of Illinois and the National

*See *Programmed Learning and Individually-Paced Instruction* Bibliography (Carl H. Hendershot; 4114 Ridgewood Drive; Bay City, Michigan 48706).
†Proceedings are available from conferences held at the University of Iowa (1970), Dartmouth College (1971), Georgia Institute of Technology (1972), and the Claremont Colleges (1973).

Science Foundation. Materials were produced first in the sciences but now extend to the social sciences, to foreign language study, and to other disciplines.

## Mastery Learning

One further outgrowth of behavioral learning theory and a systems approach to instruction is the concept of "mastery learning." In mastery learning it is assumed that 90 percent or more of the students in a class can master the subject. As in a systems approach, objectives are specified clearly and instruction is broken into incremental units. The emphasis in mastery learning is on a very thorough and systematic approach to evaluation. Specific criteria are established and students are evaluated solely with reference to the criteria.

For many college teachers this will be a new concept, since most professors are accustomed to "grading on a curve." In an essay on mastery learning, Benjamin Bloom has noted some deficiencies in grading on the curve:

> Having become "conditioned" to the normal distribution, we set grading policies in these terms and are horrified if a teacher recommends a new grading distribution. . . . The normal curve is not sacred. It describes the outcome of a random process. Since education is a purposeful activity in which we seek to have students learn what we teach, the achievement distribution should be very different from the normal curve if our instruction is effective. In fact, our educational efforts may be said to be *unsuccessful* to the extent that student achievement is normally distributed [Block, 1971, p. 49].

What is it that keeps all (or nearly all) students from mastering the subject? For one thing, it is a grading

system whereby we compare students to other students
(norm-referenced evaluation) instead of comparing student
performance to stated criteria (criterion-referenced evaluation). If the system can be changed so that students
are shooting for specified goals (instead of their neighbor's
grade point average), they will have a better chance of
knowing when they have mastered the material. According
to mastery learning theorists, the degree of learning
which takes place in most classes is a function of one
or more of five factors: (1) time allotted, (2) perseverance,
(3) aptitude, (4) quality of instruction, and (5) ability
to understand instruction (Block, 1971). If a student
is unable to master the material, the chances are he or
she needs help—more time, better instruction, or some
aid in compensating for deficiencies.

One way of assuring that the help is made available
at the right time is to do a much better job of evaluation.
Evaluation must take place at three key points: (1) at
the beginning (prospective evaluation), (2) during instruction (formative evaluation), and (3) at the end (summative
evaluation) (Block, 1971). Most college teachers today
are familiar with pretest and posttest procedures; where
we fall down is in evaluating students during the instructional process to see whether they are, in fact, learning.

One instructor at Cornell University has devised a unique
instructional feedback system for a class of 400 students.
It is an electronic student-response system which allows
students to press one of five buttons which correspond
to the "a, b, c, d, e" responses on a multiple-choice
test. The professor can stop his lecture at any point,
pose a question, and instantaneously get a count of
correct responses. The system is *not* used for quizzes
or exams. It is used for review, to engage a student's
interest at the beginning of a lecture, or to let the student
project a probable answer in a particular line of reasoning.
The student knows when he is catching on and so does
the professor. Conversely, the teacher also knows when
he has lost the whole class. If you don't have an electronic
feedback system, you might just pause in the middle

of a class, pose a multiple-choice question, and see how many students get it right.

Mastery learning is really just another application of behavioral learning theory. It assumes a systems approach to instruction and employs an evaluation system that allows the teacher to identify trouble spots quickly so that the additional resources needed to bring every student up to mastery level can be provided as needed.

## Objections Overruled

There are some fundamental criticisms that can be made of behavioral learning theory. The main issue has to do with whether the model of human learning developed by the behaviorists is sufficiently comprehensive to deal with the varieties of learning which take place in the college classroom. That issue will be addressed in succeeding chapters. But for some reason behavioral learning theory comes in for other kinds of criticism which seem not as valid, criticism that college teachers are quick to make, as if to dismiss the whole systems approach without giving it a fair hearing. Some of these objections are addressed here (Skinner, 1974; Kibler, Barker, and Miles, 1970).

It is sometimes argued that the behavioral approach is based entirely on the observation of rats, and that humans don't learn in the same ways that rats learn. Skinner has countered that objection:

> The reign of the white rat in the psychological laboratory ended at least a quarter century ago. . . . If . . . one begins with animals, the emphasis is no doubt on those features which animals and people have in common. . . . That is the direction—from simple to complex—in which science moves. But one applies the system by removing

the limits as rapidly as possible and working directly
with human behavior [Skinner, 1974, pp. 226-227].

We have seen how the patterns of human learning parallel
learning in animals. No one has argued that humans
learn in exactly the same way as animals, but there are
parallels. Behaviorists have discovered by watching animals
*and* humans some important rules that govern human
learning.

It is often argued that behaviorists are interested primarily
in the control of human behavior and that their methods
are manipulative. It is true that behaviorists are interested
in predicting and thereby controlling human behavior.
It does not follow, however, that control necessarily
has to result in evil purposes; it can lead to shared goals
of very high purpose. If students and teachers agree
about certain goals and express this agreement by gathering
together as teacher and taught in groups called classes,
it would hardly be manipulative for the teacher to try
to present a program or system which will help the student
reach the goal (complete the course) as effectively and
efficiently as possible. Manipulation often implies ex-
ploitation. If students are made aware of the educational
process they are involved in, if they share the goals
and are not being tricked or fooled, then it seems unfair
to use the words "manipulative" or "exploitive" to describe
what takes place under an instructional system grounded
in behavioral learning theory.

It is argued that a systems approach is too rigid. It is
true that the goals and the steps to these goals are fairly
well fixed in a systems approach, but the range of
learning experiences that are to be used can vary tre-
mendously. Serendipity in the classroom is always welcome,
but it ought to be justifiable in terms of its contribution
to some goal. Much that passes for creativity in the
classroom turns out to be ephemeral entertainment or
temporary diversion. It is great to discover something
new as long as everyone knows what has been discovered.

A systems approach is said to be dehumanizing and impersonal. It is unfortunate that behaviorists have been stacked against "humanists" in what is surely an unfortunate way to divide up the field of psychology. Behaviorists have developed theories and principles, a kind of technology, which can be applied toward achieving humane goals. As we have seen, one of the main goals that recurs in most instructional systems is the individualizing and personalizing of instruction so that everyone can succeed.

It is said that instructional systems put the instructor in an authoritarian role. This may be true, but most teaching strategies relegate the instructor to some role of authority. Although a college professor usually does not decide entirely on his own what the content of the curriculum is to be—there is usually some input from colleagues and students—it is true that most college teachers find themselves in the classroom because they are an "authority" on something and they have a discipline to teach. A college teacher really ought not have to apologize for setting certain goals and designing the system which will enable students to attain those goals.

It is often said that instructional systems are best able to operationalize the most trivial goals and that the really important outcomes of education are underemphasized. Too often it is true that trivial matters are the subject of complex instructional systems. That is a misfortune, but it grows out of the way the systems are used, not the systems themselves. The systems can be applied to the most important goals of education, but it may take more effort.

It is said that instructional systems only work for certain subjects; that they work best with the sciences and languages and not at all for the fine arts and humanities. It is no doubt more difficult to apply a systems strategy to the fine arts and the humanities, but it is no less possible or desirable. Though most artists, writers, and musicians have their criteria and standards of excellence, they have a tendency not to put their criteria on the line. Instruction in such areas, while difficult, could be greatly enhanced by a systems approach.

Finally, it has been said that a systems approach involves overindulgence, a kind of "spoon-feeding" that has no place in a college classroom. Skinner has some hard words to offer to those who believe in making things hard for students:

> The standard defense of "hard" material is that we want to teach more than subject matter. The student is to be challenged and taught to "think." The argument is sometimes little more than a rationalization for confusing presentation, but it is doubtless true that lectures and texts are often inadequate and misleading by design. But to what end? What sort of thinking does the student learn in struggling through difficult material? It is true that those who learn under difficult conditions are better students, but are they better because they have surmounted difficulties or do they surmount them because they are better? In the guise of teaching thinking we set difficult and confusing situations and claim credit for the students who deal with them successfully [Skinner, 1968, p. 51].

There are many arguments against behavioral learning theory and instructional systems, but most of the objections can be overruled. The principles of behavioral psychology represent a central body of theory which every educator today must confront. Even those teachers who may disagree with some of the basic principles of behaviorism will find in the systems approach a viable strategy for attacking systematically certain aspects of the task of college teaching. For those who find the systems approach incomplete, there are other strategies.

# References

Block, James H. *Mastery Learning*. New York: Holt, Reinhart and Winston, 1971.

Burns, Richard W. *New Approaches to Behavioral Objectives*. Dubuque, Iowa: Wm. C. Brown Co., 1972.

Davis, Robert H., Lawrence T. Alexander, and Stephen L. Yelon. *Learning System Design*. New York: McGraw-Hill Book Co., 1974.

Keller, Fred S. *Learning: Reinforcement Theory*. New York: Random House, 1954.

Kibler, Robert J., Larry L. Barker, and David T. Miles. *Behavioral Objectives and Instruction*. Boston: Allyn and Bacon, 1970.

Lindvall, C. M. *Defining Educational Objectives*. Pittsburgh, Penna.: University of Pittsburgh Press, 1964.

Littauer, Ralph. "The Student Response System." Unpublished paper, 1971.

Macht, Joel. *Teacher, Teachim*. New York: John Wiley & Sons, 1975a.

Macht, Joel. *Teaching Our Children*. New York: John Wiley & Sons, 1975b.

Mager, Robert F. *Preparing Instructional Objectives*. Palo Alto, Calif.: Fearon Publishers, 1962.

Milton, Ohmer. *Alternatives to the Traditional*. San Francisco: Jossey-Bass, 1972.

Skinner, B. F. *About Behaviorism*. New York: Alfred A. Knopf, 1974.

Skinner, B. F. *Science and Human Behavior*. New York: The Free Press, 1953.

Skinner, B. F. *The Technology of Teaching*. New York: Appleton-Century Crofts, 1968.

Stolurow, Lawrence. "Programmed Instruction." In Robert L. Ebel, ed., *The Encyclopedia of Educational Research*, pp. 1017-1021. London: The Macmillan Co., 1969.

Watson, John B. *Behaviorism*. New York: The People's Institute Publishing, 1924. Reprint. New York: W. W. Norton and Co., 1970.

# STRATEGY 2:
## Communicating
## Through Lectures

Most college teachers at one time or another find themselves lecturing. In recent years lecturing has been called into question. Traditional teachers lecture, it is said; while those who count themselves among the avant-garde, the innovative, and the experimental will avoid the formal lecture. This is a false and unfortunate dichotomy. Lecturing is neither inherently good nor bad. It has been and remains one of the chief strategies of the college teacher. What is wrong with lecturing is that it is so often done poorly. And it is done poorly because most college teachers don't understand the complexity involved in the transmission and reception of information. To understand the process of communication involved in lecturing it is helpful to know something about human cognitive processes generally.

## Cognitive Psychology

Critics of the behaviorists say that the model of operant conditioning is inadequate for fully describing human learning. Although learning is surely influenced by the consequences of behavior, human beings—largely because they alone have the gift of language—act upon and reorder the stimuli which constitute the environment.

Through language and other symbolization processes humans engage in complex, covert mental activity. Whereas most behaviorists would regard the human mind as a "black box" not amenable to investigation, cognitive psychologists believe that covert mental processes—the things that go on in the head—are the key to understanding human behavior.

The debate about whether cognitive processes are amenable to study has taken place for nearly a century. Some of the earliest psychology involved the study of states of consciousness. Indeed, it was a rejection of such study that gave birth to the development of the empirical science of behavior we associate with Skinner. But the study of consciousness was kept alive, against considerable behaviorist opposition, by another group of psychologists who insisted that consciousness must be studied as an entity in itself; and that its forms, patterns, and configurations must be examined in their entirety. Thus Wertheimer introduced the word "gestalt" to describe the total configuration of consciousness. His work was supplemented by that of Lewin and Tolman.

The research of cognitive psychologists today is carried on in the tradition of gestalt psychology in that it focuses on understanding covert mental processes; but it would be unfair to describe it, as behaviorists are inclined to, as not being empirical. Quite to the contrary, the work of cognitive theorists is based upon rigorous experimentation and observation, and the conclusions reached are derived from inferences about observed behavior. The chief disagreements between behavioral and cognitive psychologists have to do with whether the domain of "mental activity" is worth studying and whether models and theories can rightly be built upon "inferences" as opposed to strict scientific observation of the phenomena. The main difficulty is that most mental activity is not directly observable as overt behavior. But because one can't observe consciousness doesn't mean it is not there or not available for some kind of study. It *is* there, and cognitive psychologists think that it is worthwhile trying to study it.

## Attention Mechanisms

What transpires when a student listens to a lecture? What goes on in the head? If you are inclined to say "not much," you are wrong; cognitive psychologists have been able to describe an exceedingly complex process.

First of all, before we can assimilate any information we must attend to it. Researchers have observed that human beings seem to have amazing abilities to pay attention to an identifiable conversation or line of reasoning and to pick it out from a jumble of stimuli. In a series of experiments, subjects were asked to listen to a tape recording on which one message (Message B) had been superimposed on a previously recorded message (Message A). The results sounded like a complete jumble, but given the time and some persistence, most subjects were able to focus upon one message, identify it, and describe its content. This difficult task of sorting out one message from a variety of stimuli has been called "the cocktail party problem" (Cherry, 1957). If you have ever tried to follow one conversation at a party while three other interesting ones were going on behind your back, you know the problem: Whatever you hear in one conversation causes you to lose the others.

In another series of experiments, cognitive psychologists used binaural headphones through which one message (Message A) was sent to the left ear and a different message (Message B) was sent to the right ear. The subject was asked to "shadow" the message, that is, to repeat it aloud as soon as it was heard, staying as close behind the recorded speaker as possible. It was found

41

that subjects could easily focus their attention on one message at a time, that the attended message was comprehended, and that the rejected message was almost totally ignored (Neisser, 1966). In some instances the subjects were not even sure if the rejected message was speech, so focused was their attention on the listening task.

The reader can experience what happens in selected message/rejected message experiments by reading the shaded portions of the following paragraph (adapted from Lindsay and Norman, 1972, p. 364).

In reading a apple paragraph orange such as this, it is pear important to keep your attention peach on the assigned plum task and apricot not let your lemon mind wander lime at all.

What did you notice about the unshaded words? Did you observe that each word is a kind of fruit? What you probably noticed is that your mind focused rather precisely on the task and that the peripheral stimuli, while noticed, were not processed very well.

In 1957, D. E. Broadbent published what has become a classical model for describing human attention mechanisms. He said that human attention operates like a Y-tube with a hinged gate. In this model (Figure 2) one thinks of dropping balls through a Y-tube, the balls representing units of information stimuli. The branching arms represent various sensory channels. If two balls of equal weight are dropped simultaneously, the tube will probably jam and neither will get through. If one is dropped sooner than the other, the first will

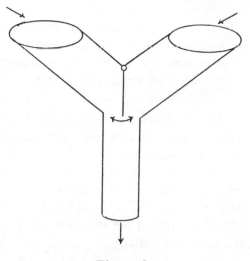

Figure 2

probably get through. If one is heavier or is flung
harder, it will probably get through. After one ball has
made its way through, the hinged gate will probably
swing back and make it more difficult for another stimulus
just like that one to come through. The point of the
model is that what human beings attend to depends
on the nature of the stimuli, their order, and their force.
When we attend to something, we attend to it almost
exclusively. More recent theories of attention have sup-
planted the billiard ball model. It is argued that attention
is not so much like a switch that is either on or off;
but rather, is more likely governed by an attenuator
mechanism, a device that simply *reduces* the amount
of information that gets past, rather than shutting it
off completely (Lindsay and Norman, 1972). In either
case, what gets in is what we attend to.

## Information Processing

What do we do with the stimuli we attend to? In recent
years, cognitive psychologists have begun to develop

coherent theories about how human beings process information. The theories have been built out of a series of principles derived from experimental evidence. Some of the basic principles are as follows:

1. *Perceptions are not isomorphic with actual stimuli.* There is not a one-to-one correspondence between our perceptions and the stimuli that produce them. We use a process of abstraction called pattern recognition or feature extraction. In other words, we act upon stimuli as they "come in," we sort out the features or chief characteristics of the stimulus and begin to group the features into patterns.

Consider Figure 3. It appears to be a diagram of a three-dimensional rectangle with a hollow center. Even though

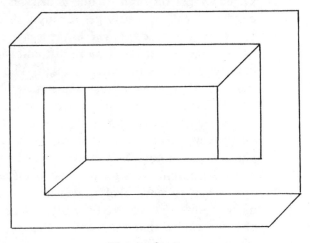

Figure 3

the lines are not in fact three-dimensional, we are familiar enough with rectangles to assign the rectangle depth and bulk. It doesn't look like rectangles we are familiar with that are "flat," so we attribute thickness to it. In our minds we associate this with other, more conventional rectangles, but it doesn't look quite "right." The planes and surfaces, the ends and edges keep misbehaving. They won't hold their proper positions no matter how hard we work to make them come out "right." We know that this is a three-dimensional rectangle with a hollow center, so we want it to do the things that other three-dimensional rectangles do, but it refuses to do so. The planes do not hold position. The top one becomes a side one, which becomes a top one again, but on the inside of the rectangle. It is clearly a deviant rectangle.

The problem we have with the figure comes from what we keep trying to do to it to make it come out "right." What we are engaged in is not a simple matter of seeing what's "out there." We see what's "out there" by working on the stimulus with what we know already, so we can see it appropriately in reference to other seeing and knowing that we do.

Some interesting examples of the way we act upon stimuli are provided by certain auditory experiments. For example, it is now possible to simulate speech on a computer. In fact, a computer can be programmed to say, "I am a computer." An intriguing question arises: When do the programmed sounds become speech? Interestingly enough, they become "speech" for different people at different times, depending on how people process the sounds. There is no one-to-one correspondence between certain vibrations produced by a computer and certain human apprehensions of those vibrations as words. "Speech" depends, in part, on what we bring to the stimuli.

Although the process of feature analysis and pattern recognition is dramatized by the deviant rectangle and the talking computer (as it is by optical illusions and various forms of op art), we actually act upon *all* stimuli in this way. Thus, "we not only believe what we see; to some extent we see what we believe" (Gregory, 1970, p. 15).

2. *Perceptions are related to a "field" or some previous experience.* Perceptions do not take place in isolation; they must be related to something familiar. The gestalt

45

psychologists documented this point years ago. Stimuli are perceived against a backdrop, ground, or field. To perceive the stimulus, one must see it in relationship to that which surrounds it. Consider, for example, Figure 4 (adapted from Lindsay and Norman, 1972, p. 28).

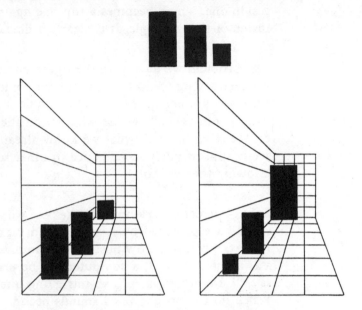

Figure 4

The three boxes, when shown alone, are clearly of three different sizes. But when they are shown in relationship to the perspective drawing, their actual sizes take on an apparent change relative to their position. What we see here with size also takes place with shape, color, intensity, or any of the other properties of an object. What we perceive an object to be is relative to its surroundings and our previous experience with those surroundings.

The point is further illustrated by a demonstration. Two sets of cards are held up before subjects for one-half second. The subjects are asked to remember the three sets of three letters which appear on each card. The first card contains the following letters:

QJB
ZBX
YKL

Subjects find it difficult to process more than one group of the letters. Then the second card is held up for the same length of time with these letters on it:

IBM
CIA
IOU

Subjects have no trouble processing all three sets of letters, because the configurations tie into familiar, existing codes already in the consciousness. The perceptions are easily made because they tie into previous experience and have a "meaning" derived from familiar surroundings and associations.

3. *Perceptions can be highly idiosyncratic.* One man's meat is another's poison. What you see and hear may not be what I see and hear. In an interesting demonstration, subjects are asked to tell what they hear from a single stimulus repeated over and over, such as "tish, tish, tish, tish . . ." The sound is electronically produced so that there is no variation in the stimulus as it is repeated. In a group of 20 or 30 persons, there may be 20 or 30 reports of what was heard, ranging from "I wish" to "fresh fish." Although human beings share a common mechanism for processing stimuli—perceptions will fall into a certain range of the possible—there is no guarantee that one individual will see things or hear things in exactly the same way that another individual does. While much of our perceiving is socially conditioned, some of it is also highly individualized and idiosyncratic.

4. *Two or more kinds of information processing can interfere.* Sometimes the system can get overloaded when too many stimuli are being processed at once. Particularly difficult are tasks in which the processing of nonverbal

visual stimuli and verbal visual stimuli conflict. The classic example is the Stroop Color Word Test. Subjects are asked to read the colors from three different charts. The first chart has rows of colored circles, and subjects find the task fairly simple. Then subjects are asked to read the colors which appear in the form of words. The color blue is printed using the letters "b-l-u-e." This goes even better, for the words and colors are processed together easily. Then the subject is asked to read the colors from words that spell different colors. For example, the color blue is used to make up the letters of the word "orange." The result is usually disastrous. Subjects stumble and halt, trying to follow the color stimulus while trying to fight off natural inclinations to read the verbal stimulus. Human beings apparently have trouble processing more than one thing at a time and have their primary orientation to verbal stimuli.

The principles described briefly above serve as a basis for a theory of information processing. There is surely no agreement among cognitive psychologists about what is the best theory. In fact, some of the most heated battles in the field are waged over identifying a model which accounts for all aspects of mental activity. A great amount of energy has been expended in experimentation with computers to simulate a human information-processing model, but without much success. Most cognitive psychologists are content with some variation of the mechanical model which appears in Figure 5. Keep in mind that the model is simply a "model," an extended metaphor used to try to help us better understand what we do with the stimuli that bombard us.

Inputs (stimuli) enter the organism from a variety of sources. Certain attention mechanisms channel them into immediate awareness. The organism acts upon the stimuli in order to extract the key features of the stimuli and order them into patterns. Then they become part of the short-term memory (echoic memory for sounds, iconic memory for images) where they are coded, reworked, symbolized, and put into forms that can be remembered

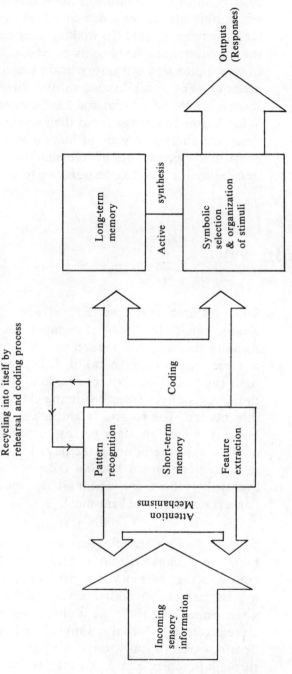

## INFORMATION PROCESSING MODEL

Recycling into itself by
rehearsal and coding process

**Inputs (Stimuli)**

Incoming sensory information

Attention Mechanisms

Pattern recognition

Short-term memory

Feature extraction

Coding

Long-term memory

Active synthesis

Symbolic selection & organization of stimuli

**Outputs (Responses)**

Figure 5

briefly. Some of the information is forgotten immediately, while other aspects of it are coded and put into long-term memory or used. In making outputs (responses) the organism uses new inputs as well as the interactions of new inputs and old information stored in long-term memory. (For a full discussion of information processing theory, see Neisser, 1966; and Lindsay and Norman, 1972). What begins to emerge from the principles and the model described above is a view of human beings as active, constructive processors of information who are acting upon stimuli as well as responding to them.

## Memory

Some researchers believe that there are at least three clearly identifiable kinds of memory. One is an "erasable" memory that allows a person to retain a telephone number long enough to call it. It acts on a short-term basis (up to five or six seconds) and may prevent the thought processes from becoming clogged with useless information. The second might be called an "agenda" memory, which allows a person to give an accounting of what happened during the day. The third is a long-term memory for intellectual skills or for important events. It is this third, or long-term, memory which concerns college teachers most.

There are a number of theories about memory, some of them more plausible than others. The popular view, of course, is that memory is a gift. We speak of having a good memory or poor memory as if memory were a given, something that one is either blessed with or not. Recent research does not support such a view. Nor does research support the idea of improving the memory through practice. Years ago the psychologist William James spent 38 days learning the first book of *Paradise Lost*. This effort, James thought, should improve his capacity to memorize. But when he tried an additional block of the same material he found that it came no more easily. He asked several friends to try the same technique, and they all agreed that there was no improvement (Norman, 1969). The notion that memory is improved by use rests on an outdated psychology of mental faculties which compares the mind to a muscle that improves with exercise. Such theories rely heavily on the equally out moded concept of transfer of training. Unfortunately, many college teachers still seem to think that students will improve their memories by having to memorize.

A more recent theory suggests that remembering and forgetting involve interference. Subjects are given lists of words to recall. The lists are longer than most subjects can readily retain—seven, plus or minus two, seems to be the maximum for most of us—and so some patterns can be discerned in what is forgotten. Psychologists have discovered that words learned previously on one list tend to interfere with the recall of words on later lists (proactive interference) and words learned on subsequent lists tend to interfere with the recall of words on lists learned earlier (retroactive interference). Furthermore, words which appear first on a list (primacy effect) and last on a list (recency effect) tend to be remembered best (Norman, 1969). Words in the middle are interfered with by the words we remember more vividly because of their placement in the list.

One theory of memory suggests that things are remembered best when they are organized into a meaningful system. The seven, plus or minus two, things we can retain can be expanded greatly by working the items into larger structures. We divide phone numbers into area codes and prefixes to aid in remembering them. Children first learn the alphabet by clustering the letters into sing-song patterns [(ab-cd) (ef-g)] [(hi-jk) (lmno-p)]. Most of us develop logical strategies to remember things (Norman, 1969). When subjects are asked to remember a series of ten zeros and ones (e.g., 1001010110), most will devise some scheme for categorizing the digits.

Some people put the numbers into threes, as we do for hundreds, thousands, millions, etc. Others package them in twos. Some picture them horizontally, some vertically, some in clusters. The point is clear that we seem to engage in some process of grouping, clustering, or categorization. If a logical structure is already present, the task is quite simple; but if a natural structure isn't there, then some categories or sets must be provided.

Another theory of memory grows out of the techniques of mnemonists, professional memory experts who perform "amazing feats of memory" before large audiences. Although psychologists have been reluctant to examine the techniques of mnemonists, in recent years their methods have been widely discussed and revealed to the public. The original "memory book," an English translation of a work by the Russian psychologist A. R. Luria, was published in 1968. It is the account of S., a Russian mnemonist, and reveals the techniques he used as a professional memory expert. Instead of ordering information into logical categories and groupings, S. engaged in bizarre and vivid associations that became truly "unforgettable." When he heard or read a word he converted it into a vivid visual image which he established in his mind. As S. described it:

> When I hear the word *green,* a green flower pot appears; with the word *red* I see a man in a red shirt coming toward me; as for *blue,* this means an image of someone waving a small blue flag from a window. . . . Even numbers remind me of images. Take the number 1. This is a proud well-built man; 2 is a high-spirited woman, 3 a gloomy person . . . 8 a very stout woman, a sack within a sack [Luria, 1968, p. 31].

The techniques of mnemonists have been discussed fully in the best seller by Lorayne and Lucas, *The Memory Book.* The basic principle is quite simple: "In order to remember any new piece of information it must be

52

associated to something you already know in some ridiculous way." The authors explain, step by step, how a series of words can be memorized in order. Assume that the list begins with "airplane," "tree," and "envelope."

> First you need a ridiculous—impossible, crazy, illogical, absurd—picture or image to associate the two items. What you don't want is a logical or sensible picture. . . . A ridiculous or impossible picture might be: a gigantic tree is flying instead of an airplane, or an airplane is growing instead of a tree, or airplanes are growing on trees, or millions of trees (as passengers) are boarding airplanes. . . . Choose a ridiculous association between airplane and tree and see it in your mind's eye, right now. . . . The next item on the list is envelope. We'll assume that you already know, or remember, tree. The new thing to remember is envelope. Simply form a ridiculous picture, or association, in your mind between tree and envelope. You might see millions of envelopes growing on a tree, or a tree is sealing a gigantic envelope, or you're trying to seal a tree in an envelope [Lorayne and Lucas, 1974, pp. 25-27].

The authors go on to suggest that associations, or links, wherever possible should be out of proportion and should involve exaggeration or action.

Although the debate about using logical or absurd associations will not be resolved easily, it does seem clear that memory is not a gift, but rather an active process whereby vivid, lasting associations are made.

## Toward a Cognitive Theory of Learning

All of this discussion, from the descriptions of the simplest attention mechanisms to the conflicting ideas about memory, suggests a theory of cognitive processes, which in turn suggests a theory of human learning. Intervening between stimulus and response is a complex organism, in the case of human beings an organism with various capabilities of symbolic representation culminating in language. As a fantastic array of stimuli present themselves we select the ones we will attend to. We pay attention to certain stimuli for certain reasons (especially if we have been told to) and begin to act upon the stimuli to put them into a form we can "hold on to." Things are not seen as they are (perceptions are not isomorphic with stimuli), and they are related to a field or to some previous experience. Perceptions can be idiosyncratic, and various types of sensory inputs can conflict in processing. The information is coded, reworked, and stored. Eventually a response is made, but only following intense and complex covert mental activity.

From this we can extrapolate a theory of human learning which is rather different from that suggested by the behaviorists. The learner is seen as an active, constructive being who is not only acted upon but acts in response to the information he receives. The more static S→R model of the behaviorists is replaced with the dynamic model of information-processing theory. Language becomes the all-important information-processing medium and communication within the individual becomes a delicate transaction between stimuli in the perceivable world and the symbols that are used to represent it.

## Implications for Teaching

What are the implications of cognitive learning theory for the college teacher who plans to lecture? How can a lecture be planned and executed to take into account what we know about the way human beings attend to, process, and remember information?

Let us assume that the topic for the day is the activity of the heart in the human circulation system. This is a unit that may come up in a basic biology course, an advanced physiology course, a health course, or a general science course. It is a topic that does not lend itself to inquiry methods or group processes, i.e., it is a good topic for a lecture.

First of all, we know that students must attend to information before they can process it. So we probably need to suggest why the topic generally is one that deserves attention. Furthermore, we need to identify in our minds, and for our students, the five or six key points or concepts that they need to attend to during the lecture. Such a topic can involve a bewildering array of concepts, terms, and illustrations; and unless students know what to pay attention to, they will miss the essentials. Students have well-developed attenuators, and they will quickly filter out the nonessentials if they are told what is essential. The teacher plays an important role in helping students to focus attention on the main ideas.

The lecturer will then need to enter into some description of the basic features of the heart. In doing so, he will be aware that students will take the information that is provided, whether through words, diagrams, pictures, or models, and will begin to extract from the material the essential features and basic patterns. An actual heart will probably not be available, nor is it necessary to have one, because understanding how the heart works involves a basic process of abstraction and symbolization. There will not be a one-to-one correspondence between the actual heart and the words and pictures used to describe it. Thus an accurate photograph or detailed visual representation of the heart may not be as helpful as a simple diagram that helps students to abstract the central features.

In describing the flow of blood through the heart it is necessary to introduce a certain amount of terminology (superior vena cava, left atrium, pulmonary artery, right ventricle, etc.). It will be important to try to tie the terms into language with which the student has had some previous experience or association. For example, a cava suggests a cave; an atrium is a small entryway. Otherwise, if too much unfamiliar terminology is introduced at once, it will appear unintelligible, like the letters QJG, ZBX, YKL on the chart mentioned on page 47. Similarly, the basic principles of blood circulation need to be related to familiar concepts and associations, perhaps principles and models drawn from the plumbing of a house or the cooling system of a car. Students will need to see the overall gestalt of the circulation system and will also need to understand where it fits among the body's other systems.

At some point an unexpected question may arise. A student may not understand some part of the illustration or may have the diagram oriented the wrong way in relation to the body. An astute lecturer will realize that this is not a "dumb question," but rather an idiosyncratic interpretation, one of many which are probably taking place out there in the heads of the students.

As the lecture proceeds it will be important for the teacher to work with one medium at a time. If materials are handed out, time should be allowed for their examination. If a slide is projected it should be discussed. A good lecturer will avoid projecting a slide that illustrates one point, handing out materials which make another point, while trying to talk about a third point.

The lecturer will also be clear in his own mind about what students should remember and should provide some assistance to students in making associations that facilitate recall. It may be pointed out that the position of the "superior" (above) vena cava and the "inferior" (below) vena cava determines their names, i.e., that there is a logical system for remembering some of the terminology. The terms associated with the heart may be grouped according to the four basic sections of the heart or perhaps by inflow and outflow functions. Or perhaps the lecturer will need to suggest some mnemonic devices, like three big teeth to help remember the tricuspid valve or a long train of pullman cars headed out to the lungs to remember the pulmonary artery.

Throughout the whole lecture the teacher will want to keep in mind that students are active processors of information. As they listen and look they will be searching for essential features and basic patterns. The notes they take are codes for what they perceive, and the teacher may want to provide outlines, perhaps as handouts, to insure that the coding process is orderly and complete. Students will follow only what they attend to and they will remember only those things that have become, for some reason, unforgettable. The rest is mere words, words that drift out over the classroom and fall unattended to the floor.

Teachers who take into account the way the mind works will be far more effective than those who just stand up and talk. Lecturing is part art but mostly science. Those who employ lecturing as a teaching strategy need to recognize it for what it is, a highly complex mode of transmitting and receiving information. For most college teachers, lecturing is like throwing the shot: They spend all their time getting together a very heavy message and then they just fling it. Lecturing, in fact, is more like throwing a frisbee: The message has to be thrown in such a way that it can be caught and with some reasonable expectation that it can be returned.

# References

Broadbent, D. E. "A Mechanical Model for Human Attention and Immediate Memory." *Psychological Review,* 64:3 (1957), 206 ff.

Cherry, Colin. *On Human Communication.* New York: John Wiley and Sons, 1957.

Gregory, R. L. *The Intelligent Eye.* New York: McGraw-Hill Book Co., 1970.

Lindsay, Peter, and Don Norman. *Human Information Processing: An Introduction to Psychology.* New York: Academic Press, 1972.

Lorayne, Harry, and Jerry Lucas. *The Memory Book.* New York: Stein and Day, 1974.

Luria, Aleksandr R. *The Mind of a Mnemonist.* New York: Basic Books, 1968.

Neisser, Ulric. *Cognitive Psychology.* New York: Appleton-Century-Crofts, 1966.

Norman, Donald A. *Memory and Attention.* New York: John Wiley & Sons, 1969.

# STRATEGY 3:
## *Facilitating Inquiry*

"But we are here to teach them to think! They aren't just memory machines. They aren't jugs to be filled with the so-called facts. The world is confronted by problems today that threaten our very existence. Unless we graduate some people who can solve these problems, we're all doomed. The goal is the inquiring mind, remember?"

You can probably recall some variation of that little tirade in the peculiar form that it was delivered on your campus by a colleague, dean, or president. But it is more than a tirade. Something rings true in the clichés. We are here to "teach them to think." But whatever does it mean to teach someone to *think?*

## Thinking about Thinking

There is a long history of thinking about thinking. The thought processes have been the object of speculation since before the time of Aristotle. For the most part, such reflection has been the province of philosophers, but in recent times, thinking has become a field of study for psychologists and linguists as well. As might be expected, there are some heated debates about what takes place when a person "thinks." In fact, it is even difficult to define what is meant by thinking.

In an effort to arrive at a definition of thinking we might ask: Is man the only animal capable of thinking? The question is not necessarily answered in the affirmative. In a classical experiment done by Hunter (1913), various animals were placed in a start box where they could view three light bulbs, one of which was lit and baited with food. After the light was turned off the animals were kept in the box for several seconds before being released. Thus they had to "think about" and "remember" where to go. Hunter found that rats could remember where to go for about 10 seconds, cats for 18 seconds, dogs for 3 minutes, a two-and-one-half-year-old child for 50 seconds, and a five-year-old child for 20 minutes or more.

In a more complex problem animals were given an opportunity to see food through a U-shaped wire screen, but in order to get the food were required to move back away from the food and take a roundabout route around the U-shaped barrier. Dogs can solve the problem, but not rats (McGaugh, 1974).

The results of some of the earliest studies of "thinking" in higher animals were published after World War I by Wolfgang Köhler (1925) in a book entitled *The Mentality of Apes*. Köhler presented apes with problems to solve and the means to solve the problems; it was up to the ape to come up with the solution. For example, Kohler tied a banana high out of reach in the ape's cage; but he also gave the ape some boxes to use to get the banana. The ape would try various ways to get at the banana and then would appear to give up on the problem. He would go sit in one corner of the cage to "think" it over. After a few minutes he would crawl over to the boxes, stack them on top of each other, climb up, and get the banana. Again and again Köhler would note what seemed to be a mental process which seemed to involve "insight" or "thinking."

Can animals think? If we mean by "thinking," the solution of some elementary problems, it appears that some animals can think. On the other hand, the level of conceptualization in animals appears to be rather limited. Animals seem to lack the important attribute which sets man apart as a unique being—the gift of language.

Many animals have some form of intraspecies communication. For example, the female Bombyx moth, when ready to mate, releases an odor that can be detected as much as seven miles away by the male. And the male, by responding differentially to different levels of concentration of the odor, can find her (McGaugh, 1974). Now that's communication! But it does not involve language. Language involves words. Language has grammar and syntax. It includes a symbolization process that enables man to hold and manipulate concepts. So far, man seems to be the only species capable of language. Or is he? In a fascinating longitudinal study Hayes and Hayes (1951) raised a chimp named Vicki from birth to age six in their home. They tried to teach Vicki to speak, but the results were negative—four words not clearly pronounced. But could Vicki understand, if not speak? In another experiment Gardner and Gardner (1969) taught an ape named Washoe to use sign language. Washoe learned a vocabulary of 100 words and used the signs appropriately in a variety of situations. She even "spoke" six-word sentences.

Can apes speak? Not very well. Can they think? Some, perhaps. But what they lack is the ability to use *language* to *think*. That seems to be uniquely human. Most psychologists and linguists would agree on one point: Thought and language are closely interwoven in man. Thinking is accompanied by the use of language. (Unfortunately, the reverse is not always the case.)

What we mean by "thinking," then, is the ability to
form a concept of something, to examine and ponder
the concept, to join the concept to others in order to
cogitate, to meditate, and to reason. Thinking involves
the ability to imagine, devise, or contrive a solution
to a problem. It is a process that involves the manipulation of mental images and symbols and as such grows
out of man's capabilities to use language.

## Thinking and Reasoning

Thinking has often been identified with reasoning and
reasoning with logic. The formal methods of reasoning
have been broken into two major categories, inductive
and deductive logic. Inductive logic involves the development of general laws or principles from a series of
concrete instances or examples. Deductive logic involves
the analysis of propositions and the development of
proofs to establish or disprove a statement. The psychologist and philosopher Max Wertheimer makes the
following distinction between inductive and deductive
reasoning. In induction, the emphasis is on "gathering
facts, on studying the empirically constant connections
of facts, of changes, and on observing the consequences
of changes introduced into factual situations, procedures
which culminate in general assumptions." Deduction,
on the other hand, is concerned with "the criteria that
guarantee exactness, validity, consistency of general concepts, propositions, inferences and syllogisms"
(Wertheimer, 1959, pp. 5-7).

Wertheimer goes on to point out that both systems
of logic have little to do with the actual reasoning
processes that seem to take place when human beings
try to solve problems. Induction and deduction are
after-the-fact systems to establish the truth of propositions. As other philosophers have noted, formal logic

is only a small branch of a much larger theory of inquiry. Inductive and deductive systems, whether Aristotelian or modern, all tend to limit the scope of logic to the forms of finished arguments. They fail to examine the types of thinking of which formal arguments are the result. Philosophers who think about thinking tend to emphasize the proofs which establish the outcome of productive thinking. Psychologists who think about thinking seem to be more interested in the processes involved in various modes of inquiry (Kneller, 1966).

## The Pattern of Inquiry

What are the processes that take place when a person "thinks" in order to solve a problem? Do any patterns emerge? Most attempts to identify the patterns of productive inquiry delineate certain stages. First of all, the inquirer becomes aware of a problem, a situation that calls for some sort of answer or solution. The early stages of inquiry usually focus on problem-definition. What precisely is the problem? Why is it a problem? To whom is it a problem? As the problem is defined, the inquirer begins to search for pertinent facts. What is the information that might be regarded as relevant to the problem? As the facts are gathered, the problem is usually redefined or reformulated.

Next, the inquirer begins to make a series of more or less concrete proposals. Will this work? Will that work? What if we try this? As proposals are developed they are tested on a trial and error basis. Gradually the inquirer begins to learn from his errors. "Such learning from errors plays as great a role in the solution-process as in everyday life. While the simple realization, that something does not work, can lead only to some variation of the old method, the realization of *why* it does not work, the recognition of the ground of the conflict, results in a correspondingly definite variation which corrects the recognized defect" (Duncker, 1945, p. 37). In the trial and error method there may be "good" errors and "stupid" errors (Henle, 1962). The important thing is for the inquirer to discover why the "stupid" errors are "stupid."

Eventually, through trial and error, the inquirer begins to reduce the possibilities. If an impasse is encountered, new solutions must be imagined and projected. New solutions are difficult to generate. They are more than simple associations. They may seem entirely absurd or outlandish at first blush. As one study notes, "productive thinking is impossible if the individual is chained to the past" (Birch and Rabinowitz, 1951, p. 45). Previous experience may have a negative effect on productive thinking. Problem-solving depends, at least in part, on the inquirer's ability to generate unusual solutions that are, despite their uniqueness, somehow relevant.

Throughout the trial and error stage an abstraction process is employed, whereby the inquirer tries to develop general principles for categorizing errors and generating solutions. The general properties of a solution slowly emerge. Sometimes the solution is felt and "known" before it can be put into words. Polanyi has described this "knowing without being able to say" as the "tacit dimension" of thinking (Polanyi, 1966).

Through it all there is some reasoning but also a great deal of guessing and intuition. Ulrich Neisser (1963) makes the distinction between reason and intuition as follows:

> Some judgments and decisions seem to be "rational," "logical" in that the person who makes them can explain the basis of his judgment, to himself or to another person. Others—hunches, guesses, feelings— are of obscure origin. Intuition is quick, and often compelling; reason is plodding and pale. Some persons are said to be more intuitive than others; women

perhaps more than men. Intuition plays a prominent part in interpersonal relations, in our judgments of other people and our behavior towards them. . . . One may feel inexplicably certain that a particular line of attack will yield the solution to a problem. . . . Mental processes of this kind seem to be common wherever there are situations too complex for ready logical analysis [p. 308].

Actually, intuition is an integral part of the process of inquiry, so that in actual practice there is an interplay of intuition and reason.

John Dewey (1933) summed it all up years ago in what remains a classic description of how we think:

There is no single and uniform power of thought, but a multitude of different ways in which specific things—things observed, remembered, heard of, read about—evoke suggestions or ideas that are pertinent to a problem or question and that carry the mind forward to a justifiable conclusion. Training is that development of curiosity, suggestion, and habits of exploring and testing, which increases sensitiveness to questions and love of inquiry into the puzzling and unknown; which enhances the fitness of suggestions that spring up in the mind, and controls their succession in a developing and cumulative order; which makes more acute the sense of the force, the *proving* power, of every fact observed and suggestion employed. Thinking is not a separate mental process: it is an affair of the *way* in which the vast multitude of objects that are observed and suggested are employed, the way they run together and are *made* to run together, the way they are handled. Consequently, any subject, topic, question, is intellectual not *per se* but because of the part it is made to play in directing thought in the life of any particular person.

For these reasons, the problem of *method* in forming habits of reflective thought is the problem of establishing *conditions* that will arouse and guide *curiosity;* of setting up the connections in things experienced that will on later occasions promote the flow of *suggestions,* create problems and purposes that will favor *consecutiveness* in the succession of ideas [p. 617].

## Inquiry as Teaching Strategy

How shall we establish conditions that arouse curiosity? What strategy shall we use to foster inquiry? Is it possible to teach people to think by guiding the process of inquiry?

In what is, to date, surely the most fully developed exploration of inquiry as a teaching strategy, Neil Postman and Charles Weingartner argue that the science of asking questions ought to be the chief content of the curriculum. In their book, *Teaching As a Subversive Activity,* Postman and Weingartner (1969) make a strong case for throwing out curricula and courses (including lectures) in order to get down to the more fundamental task of inquiry. Teaching, they argue, ought to involve students in the process by which knowledge is produced.

Consider, for example, where "knowledge" comes from. It isn't just *there* in a book, waiting for someone to come along and "learn" it. Knowledge is produced in response to questions. Here is the point: *Once you have learned how to ask questions—relevant and appropriate and substantial questions—you have learned how to learn and no one can keep you from learning whatever you want or need to know [p. 23].*

How does one go about teaching people to ask questions? First of all, as teachers, we have to talk less. Unless we talk less, students won't have a chance to ask questions. They won't have the opportunity to solve problems, develop their curiosity, and begin to inquire deeply into a subject. For at least part of the hour, we must stop talking. When we do talk, we should probably help our students to ask questions by asking questions, too, rather than always giving them answers.

Secondly, we need to help students understand the central role of language in thinking and develop in them some facility in the use of language. As Postman and Weingartner note:

> almost all of what we customarily call "knowledge" is language. Which means that the key to understanding a "subject" is to understand its language. In fact, that is a rather awkward way of saying it, since it implies that there is such a thing as a "subject" which contains "language." It is more accurate to say that what we call a subject *is* its language. . . . What is biology (for example) other than words? If all the words that biologists use were subtracted from the language, there would be no "biology. . . ." This means, of course, that every teacher is a language teacher [1969, p. 102].

Thirdly, we must let a line of inquiry go where it will. We may have some idea of the kinds of issues that we hope will be explored, but for inquiry to be free, it has to pursue its own end. It is crucial for students to be able to see how one thing leads to another, how and why options are tried and discarded, how general principles evolve, and how conclusions are reached. This means that a lesson will seldom have the same outcome, because different people will reach different conclusions. It's not a neat process.

Finally, a teacher who uses an inquiry strategy will be less concerned about what students learn than about *how* students learn. The "test" of their learning will not be how many facts they have learned, but how they have enhanced their ability to inquire. In observing students, the teacher will want to examine "the frequency with which they ask questions; the increase in the relevance and cogency of their questions; the frequency and conviction of their challenges to assertions made by other students or teachers or textbooks; the relevance and clarity of the standards on which they base their challenges; their willingness to suspend judgments when they have insufficient data; their willingness to modify or otherwise change their position when data warrant such change; the increase in their skill in observing, classifying, generalizing, etc.; the increase in their tolerance for diverse answers; their ability to apply generalizations, attitudes, and information to novel situations" (Postman and Weingartner, 1969, p. 36). In short, the college teacher who uses an inquiry strategy has to learn how to become a master at helping people learn how to think.

## Implications for Teaching

What would a typical college class be like where the instructor is using an inquiry strategy? What do the students typically do? What is the role of the teacher?

Let us look in on a freshman literature class. The course has included a unit on the short story and the novel. It is time to introduce the unit on poetry. The instructor passes around copies of an eight-line poem and defines the task. "Your job is to interpret the poem. I'll be a resource to you and I will help guide your inquiry into the meaning of the poem. I'll provide some factual information if you call on me for it, but I won't interpret the poem; that's your task."

The class begins to focus on the text of the poem:

> A route of evanescence,
> With a revolving wheel;
> A resonance of emerald,
> A rush of cochineal;
> And all the blossoms on the bush
> Adjust their tumbled heads;
> The mail from Tunis, probably—
> An easy morning's ride.

At first there is some moaning and groaning about how hard the poem is and how ridiculous poetry is. Then someone asks, "What about the fifty-cent words? Will you tell us what they mean? Like 'evanescence' and 'cochineal'?"

Someone in the class knows that "evanescence" is the noun form of "evanescent," which means "fleeting"— "here today and gone tomorrow," "always changing." No one knows the meaning of cochineal, so the instructor provides it: "a reddish color, like the shell of the same name." "Tunis," everyone agrees, is in North Africa.

"Is this the whole poem?" someone asks.

"What difference does it make?" someone counters.

"A lot. We can't interpret it if it's only part of a poem."

The instructor assures them that it is a whole poem.

"Is it a real poem?"

There are snickers. "As opposed to what, an unreal poem? It's a poem, all right."

"But did a real poet write it, and is it in a book some-where, or did someone just scribble out eight lines?"

"Oh come on, what difference does it make? If you wrote it, it would still be a poem, wouldn't it?"

"Maybe not. I'd feel better if I knew who wrote it. I want to know if it's a famous poet."

The instructor asks the class whether it is important to know who wrote the poem. There is a brief argument, but a majority of the class want to know who the author is.

"It's by Emily Dickinson."

"Oh, big help. Thanks a lot. Aren't we glad we know?"

"Wait a minute. I did a term paper in high school on Emily Dickinson. I love her poetry. She was a spinster who lived in New England in the middle of the 19th century. She wrote about nature, little things, like things in her garden. And she had a secret love affair."

"Aha! Secret love letters from Tunis."

"Probably."

"Probably not, in this poem."

"Wait a minute. What are we supposed to be doing . . . Emily Dickinson's biography or an interpretation of the poem?"

"An interpretation, but sometimes it helps to know . . ."

"Or maybe it doesn't. If it's *my* interpretation . . ."

"But it's *her* poem."

The instructor suggests that both points of view may be important and urges the class to examine the poem itself, its words, perhaps its form.

"It seems like there are a lot of simple words intermingled with the fifty-cent words."

"There are color words and sound words. How can you have a resonance of emerald? How can something sound green?"

"And how can you have a rush of red?"

"Is it blood?"

"There are a lot of R-words: 'route,' 'revolving,' 'resonance,' 'rush.' Is that an accident or is there a reason for that?"

"The first four lines seem to go together and then the next two, but I don't know what to do with the last two."

The instructor notes that the last two lines do seem to be set apart and commends the class for its observations. Someone wants the poem read, so the teacher reads it out loud. There is a long silence.

"I've got it! It's a mail truck. The truck is coming up this winding road and . . ."

"Hey, dumbo, there weren't any trucks in the middle of the 19th century, remember?"

"Okay, okay, a carriage. As it zips by the flowers all kind of pull back and adjust . . . and . . ."

"A love letter from Tunis, no doubt."

"But it wouldn't be an easy morning's ride in a carriage. It would take weeks. And you'd need a boat."

"Another good theory meets another good fact."

"I still think it's a mail truck."

The instructor points out that the idea of a mail carriage is a hypothesis and that what the class was doing was testing that hypothesis against the images in the poem. In general, that is probably a productive line of inquiry. Some other hypotheses are offered.

"I think it's life."

"Life? What do you mean?"

"A lot of the world's religions have said that life is a revolving wheel. The red and the green are life colors, like the blood of animals and the green of plants."

"And the mail from Tunis?"

"Well, if you stand above the earth, like an astronaut, and let the earth spin, it would be an easy morning's ride."

"Oh, come on, that's too . . . too far out."

More snickers. The instructor asks how they can tell when an interpretation is too far out.

"When it uses the words too abstractly; when the interpretation is too far from the words of the poem."

"I think one interpretation is just as good as another."

"So do I. Who can say that it's not life, or a mail carriage, or a sunset on the beach?"

"Sunset?"

"Yeah, I think it's a sunset. It makes me feel like I'm watching a sunset on a beach."

"On the fourth of July?"

"If it's the fourth of July for you, fine. Everybody has their own interpretation."

The instructor asks if some interpretations might be better than others. Could this be, for example, a poem about a basketball game? Almost everyone agrees that it is not. The instructor asks what criteria can be used to determine whether one interpretation is better than another.

"I think it's the words. You have to be able to account for all the words and images. We need to stick with the words."

The instructor suggests that that is probably a profitable line of inquiry and asks what would happen if the class worked on the first line for a while.

"What is a route of evanescence?"

"It's a route that keeps changing."

"That eliminates all permanent routes like roads and trails."

"What sorts of things go on a route of evanescence?"

"It's either a boat or something that flies."

"I think we should eliminate the boat. All the other images are from nature. The mail might come on a boat, but not in a morning."

"What things fly?"

The instructor praises them for getting "tough-minded" with the words.

"Birds."

"Maybe this is a bird. As the bird darts by, the blossoms on the bush have to adjust."

"But what about the revolving wheel?"

"Propellers."

"Not on a bird, and not in the 19th century."

"Oh, I see it! It's fantastic when you see it. It's a hummingbird."

"The red and the green."

"The rush . . . all those 'R-words' humming at you."

"But what about the mail?"

"She's being playful. They fly 120 m.p.h. She's joking. They could probably bring the mail in from Tunis."

"You won't believe this, but I did a paper on humming-birds once, and they migrate to North Africa."

"You're kidding!"

"I still think it's a mail truck."

The instructor cuts off the inquiry. "You will all have to decide whether you think it is a hummingbird or a mail truck. You will also have to decide why you think one interpretation is better than another and what criteria can be used to make that judgment. In the process of this morning's inquiry you have uncovered the poet's essential tools. You have learned how to approach a poem, what to look for, how to generate hypotheses and how to test them. You've also uncovered two or three theories of criticism which we will talk about later. Read the four poems by Dickinson in your text tonight to see if the line of inquiry you've pursued this morning helps you in reading other poems. You've worked hard; that's enough for today."

## Some Pros and Cons

Inquiry, as a teaching strategy, is unsurpassed if the goal is to teach people "to think." There is no substitute for the hard work involved in solving a problem. The only way to learn to think is to do it, over and over again, in different fields, with different problems, and with different words. The steps involved in solving a math problem are not unlike the steps involved in working out an interpretation to a poem. The words and symbols are different, the tools are different, the issues and criteria are different, but the process is essentially the same. To learn the process one must practice it.

Inquiry has its limitations, of course. It is slow. It involves reinventing the wheel. It is "inefficient" in a sense. And often it will be resisted, because it involves such hard work. It is not the best way to convey information.

But if the goal is the inquiring mind, inquiry is surely the best strategy. If a personal testimony is of any value, I have conducted over fifteen inquiry classes using Emily Dickinson's subtle poem about the hummingbird, and I've always found it nearly impossible to get the discussion stopped. Each time something "new" about the poem is uncovered, and each time there are those who shake their head and say, "I never thought about poetry like that." The last time I used the poem a student came up to me after class and said, "That inquiry business is dynamite . . . pure dynamite!"

## References

Birch, H. G., and H. S. Rabinowitz. "The Negative Effect of Previous Experience on Productive Thinking." *Journal of Experimental Psychology,* 41 (1951): 121-125. Also in Wason, P. C., and P. N. Johnson-Laird, eds., *Thinking and Reasoning, Selected Readings.* Middlesex, England: Penguin Books, 1968.

Dewey, John. *Intelligence in the Modern World.* Edited by Joseph Ratner. New York: The Modern Library, 1939. The selection is originally from John Dewey, *How We Think,* rev. ed., pp. 35-37. New York: D. C. Heath and Co., 1933.

Duncker, K. "On Problem Solving." 1945, *Psychological Monographs,* 58 (1945): 270. Also in P. C. Wason and P. N. Johnson-Laird, eds., *Thinking and Reasoning, Selected Readings.* Middlesex, England: Penguin Books, 1968.

Gardner, R. A., and B. T. Gardner. "Teaching Sign Language to a Chimpanzee." *Science,* 165 (1969): 664-672. Reported in James L. McGaugh, *Learning and Memory: An Introduction.* San Francisco: Albion Publishing Co., 1974.

Hayes, K. J., and C. Hayes. *The Ape in Our House.* New York: Harper, 1951. Reported in James L. McGaugh, *Learning and Memory: An Introduction.* San Francisco: Albion Publishing Co., 1974.

Henle, M. "On the Relation Between Logic and Thinking." *Psychological Review,* 69 (1962): 366-378. Also in Wason, P. C., and P. N. Johnson-Laird, eds., *Thinking and Reasoning, Selected Readings.* Middlesex, England: Penguin Books, 1968.

Hunter, W. S. "The Delayed Reaction in Animals and Children." *Behavior Monographs,* 2 (1913): 1-86. Reported in James L. McGaugh, *Learning and Memory: An Introduction.* San Francisco: Albion Publishing Co., 1974.

Kneller, George F. *Logic and Language of Education.* New York: John Wiley & Sons, 1966.

Köhler, Wolfgang. *The Mentality of Apes.* New York: Harcourt Brace, 1925. Reported in James L. McGaugh, *Learning and Memory: An Introduction.* San Francisco: Albion Publishing Co., 1974.

McGaugh, James L. *Learning and Memory: An Introduction.* San Francisco: Albion Publishing Co., 1974.

Neisser, U. "The Multiplicity of Thought." *British Journal of Psychology,* 54 (1963): 1-14. Also in P. C. Wason and P. N. Johnson-Laird, eds., *Thinking and Reasoning, Selected Readings.* Middlesex, England: Penguin Books, 1968.

Polanyi, Michael. *The Tacit Dimension.* New York: Doubleday & Co., 1966.

Postman, Neil, and Charles Weingartner. *Teaching As A Subversive Activity.* New York: Delacorte Press, 1969.

Wason, P. C., and P. N. Johnson-Laird, eds., *Thinking and Reasoning, Selected Readings.* Middlesex, England: Penguin Books, 1968.

Wertheimer, Max. *Productive Thinking.* New York: Harper & Row, 1959.

# STRATEGY 4:
## Utilizing Group Processes

There is more to education than thinking and reasoning. As Shakespeare has written, "The heart has its reasons, of which reason has no knowledge." Some learning involves the change of opinions and attitudes, the re-working of beliefs, and the development of a sense of values. Such "learning" is as much a matter of the heart as of the head; it involves what college catalogs call "the whole person."

College professors have been reluctant to enter this sphere. We teach in an atmosphere which stresses cognitive growth and intellectual development. It is often said, "We are not here to tamper with people's attitudes and values; we're here to present the facts." The assumption is that human beings are essentially rational, and that when given the facts, people will draw rational conclusions. The role of the professor is to present the evidence in a free and open academic environment; the role of the student is to shape his or her own opinions and beliefs based on the facts.

In recent years we have learned that the matter is not quite that simple. The relationship of evidence and opinion is more subtle than it appears on the surface. A great amount of research on what social scientists call opinions, attitudes, and beliefs (OAB) was done following World War II, and some fairly definite conclusions can be drawn. The results of that research have been summarized and reported by Berelson and Steiner in *Human Behavior: An Inventory of Scientific Findings.*

Their central point is that "people hold OABs (opinions, attitudes and beliefs) in harmony with their group memberships and identifications." OABs are rooted in group behavior. They grow out of social contacts and group affiliations. "The more homogeneous the social environment of the individual, the more intensely he holds his OABs and the more likely he is to act on them." If personal contact in the group is high, the more likely it is that people will agree on OABs. In other words, opinions, attitudes, and beliefs are not so much the product of individual thinking as of social relationships (Berelson and Steiner, 1964).

It is not surprising to find that OABs are not easily changed; and when they are changed, it is, once again, through group affiliations. "There appears to be little lasting development of OABs that is independent of parental, group, or strata dispositions and is based on 'objective' or 'rational' analysis of information and ideas." In fact "the more a person is emotionally involved in his beliefs, the harder it is to change him by argument or propaganda—that is, through an appeal to intelligence—to the point of virtual impossibility." Given consistent support from historical, parental, group, and strata characteristics, OABs are unlikely to change at all. "When OABs do change, it is through the influence of a reference group, perhaps a new affiliation. Within a group OABs are subject to influence by the most prestigious members of the group. Dissenters are inclined to join the majority, not *vice versa.*" People less interested in a matter are more likely to change their minds. OABs change more slowly than actual behavior (Berelson and Steiner, 1964, p. 557ff).

Why are groups so "persuasive" when opinions, attitudes, and beliefs are being examined? In research done by Kurt Lewin to discover the influence of various methods on learning and social change it was demonstrated that group methods produce a higher quality of results and more acceptance by the group. That is to say, groups tend to generate more and better information, and the members are more inclined to accept the outcome when they have the opportunity to discuss it in a group (Lewin, 1943). Irving Lorge and his colleagues noted that in general the products produced by groups are superior to those produced by individuals. The proponents of "brain-storming," a group problem-solving method, claim that "ideation" (the having of ideas) is 60 percent to 90 percent greater for groups than for individuals (Lorge et al., 1958). In cataloging the social-psychological research which describes the influence a group has on a person, Ladd Wheeler (1970) concluded that the presence of others has a profound effect on the norms, standards, values, and behavior of individuals. Emile Durkheim, the eminent sociologist, noted years ago that "individual ideas are altered in the process of 'psyche-social-synthesis' that goes on in groups, and that thus a group product emerges that cannot be explained in terms of individual mental processes" (Knowles and Knowles, 1959, p. 17). It seems fairly clear that learning which will alter opinions, attitudes, and beliefs will be best facilitated through groups.

Some professors will eschew any responsibility for influencing their students' opinions, attitudes, and beliefs. That, of course, is a professor's privilege. Other professors, however, regard attitude formation and the development of a sense of values as a central and important part of their task. Although most professors will clearly renounce indoctrination as a technique, many would, nevertheless, welcome the opportunity to influence their students openly in the development of humane values such as tolerance, honesty, liberality, and compassion. Those academicians who are willing to take a stand for such old-fashioned virtues must come to terms with a central principle: Opinions, attitudes, and beliefs are rooted in *group* behavior.

## Groups

People, throughout recorded history, have affiliated with other people in groups. "First in the family, then the clan, the tribe, the guild, the community, and the state, groups have been used as instruments of government, work, fighting, worship, recreation and education" (Knowles and Knowles, 1959, p. 15). Groups are not new. Formal and informal groups of various sorts are the mainstay of every society. But formal groups have become, perhaps, more important in our society now than in the past. Businesses, industries, social agencies, and educational institutions at all levels use groups and committees to improve communication and formulate and carry out policy (Phillips, 1973). One argument for employing group methods as a teaching strategy is that today's graduates cannot function in our society without knowing something about group behavior.

The conscious use of formal groups to achieve a variety of purposes—from managerial decision-making to therapy—is a fairly recent phenomenon, however. In the summer of 1946 Kurt Lewin and his colleagues were asked to train a group of community leaders to implement more effectively the Connecticut Fair Employment

Practices Act. Small group "training sessions" were used, and they included feedback reports on group behavior. In 1947 a meeting was held in Bethel, Maine, to explore ways of learning about group processes, and the next year the term "t-group" (basic skill training group) was coined. In 1949 the National Training Laboratories (NTL) was formed under the auspices of the National Education Association. Today NTL has over 65 full-time professional and administrative staff members and a network of over 600 NTL-trained group leaders (Verny, 1974). Meanwhile, another phase of the movement toward the use of formal groups was underway at the University of Chicago under the direction of Carl Rogers. Rogers developed group training techniques in a project designed to teach Veterans Administration personnel to become effective counselors (Rogers, 1970). Although the term "group therapy" was coined as far back as 1920 by J. L. Moreno (Verny, 1974), "the modern, swinging, 'let it all hang out' encounter group appeared only as a speck on the horizon before the early 1960s" (Lieberman, 1973, p. 5). It was in the '60s, and chiefly on the West Coast, that the group encounter movement began to grow. "The encounter group became a social oasis where people could drop the facade of competence demanded by a fast-moving, competitive society, and let loose their doubts and fears and disappointments" (Lieberman, 1973, p. 5). The movement was stimulated by the work and writings of Fritz Perls and Eric Berne. Today, formal groups of all sorts are accepted and utilized for a variety of purposes.

## Types of Groups

What is a group? Unfortunately, many people think only of the "let it all hang out" encounter group when they think of groups today. Burton (1969) has defined encounter groups "as 'soul' groups, in which the basic parameters of the human condition are opened for all persons to share. There is no agenda. What purpose there is is merely to live more fully and to experience more deeply." While such groups have their place and value, there are also many other kinds of groups which have very different purposes.

Malcolm and Hulda Knowles offer some helpful criteria for defining a group:

> A collection of people is a group when it possesses these qualities:
>
> 1. A definable membership—a collection of two or more people identifiable by name or type.
>
> 2. Group consciousness—the members think of themselves as a group, have a "collective perception of unity," a conscious identification with each other.
>
> 3. A sense of shared purpose—the members have the same "object model" or goal or ideals.
>
> 4. Interdependence in satisfaction of needs—the members need the help of one another to accomplish the purposes for which they joined the group.
>
> 5. Interaction—the members communicate with one another, influence one another, react to one another.
>
> 6. Ability to act in a unitary manner—the group can behave as a single organism [1959, pp. 39-40].

Thus a group may vary in size (from two people, upward), purpose, function, and process.

Most lists of the various types of formal groups usually include the following (Rogers, 1970; Barbour and Goldberg, 1974):

> *T-Group.* Intended to emphasize human relations and communications skills.
>
> *Encounter Group.* For personal growth and development through an experiential process.

*Sensitivity Training Group.* Comparable to t-groups and encounter groups.

*Task Group.* Has a specific task or project, as a committee.

*Creativity Workshop.* Focus is on creativity through some art form or medium.

*Sensory Awareness Group.* Emphasis is on body awareness through dance, touch, massage, etc.

*Organizational Development Group.* Focus is on development of leadership skills and organizational communication.

*Team Building Group.* Used in industry to develop closely knit and effective working teams.

*Gestalt Group.* Like an encounter group, but the focus is on one individual at a time in the here and now.

*Fantasy Group.* Sharing of personal fantasies, day-dreams, and free associations of the mind.

*Synanon Group.* Employs almost violent attacks on the defenses of participants.

*Creative Dramatics and Sociodrama.* Participants play roles and act out a situation that usually involves conflict or disagreement.

*Case Study Group.* Focus is on finding a resolution to a problem posed in a case history, usually of an organization or institution.

*Problem-Solving Group.* Goal is to solve a problem through brainstorming, ideal solution, or DELPHI techniques.

*Games.* Competitive "serious" activities which usually simulate a real-life problem or situation.

*Public Discussion.* Exploration of a controversial issue through round tables, panels, interviews, symposia, colloquia, or forums.

*Leaderless or Instrumented Group.* Use of a written statement, problem, puzzle, or some other stimulus to initiate group response.

The range of group techniques and processes now available is very broad. The college teacher will want to consider which techniques are best suited to the particular kind of learning being fostered. Not all group methods are relevant to the college classroom, but many, with some adaptation, are very useful.

## Stages and Phases

Most groups, whatever the type, go through various phases or stages. It takes a while for a group to become a "group," to develop an identity and become productive. The life-cycle of groups has been the object of much research, and most people who study group behavior agree that groups pass through several phases or stages.

One review of the development of groups (Gibbard et al., 1974) suggests that groups pass through the following stages of development:

1. A stage of testing and dependence, the *"forming"* of the group.
2. A stage of intragroup conflict and emotional expression, the *"storming"* of the group.
3. A stage of group cohesion, the *"norming"* of the group.
4. A stage of functional role-relatedness, the *"performing"* of the group task.

Others suggest that a three-phase development ensues where the group focuses on dependency, power, and intimacy. Still others would add a separation phase at the end, where the group works out its own dissolution when its purposes are complete. Whether one supports a linear, life-cycle, or pendular view of group development, it seems clear that most groups go through some stages. College teachers who employ group processes should be aware of and watch for such stages, and should recognize that certain kinds of behavior manifest in a group may be the result of some natural, developmental growing pains.

## Group Watching

The interactions within a group are often subtle and complex. The behavior of individuals within a group has been the object of intense study in recent years, and people who know what to look for can identify a variety of patterns. Most of the literature on group interaction divides group processes into two main categories, those related to the group's task and those related to the interpersonal or "socio-emotional" needs of the individuals who make up the group (Bales, 1950).

Much of a group's behavior focuses on its task, i.e., its purposes, goals, and functions. Most groups have a job to do, whether the job be educational, managerial, or therapeutic, so some of its members' behavior will be "task-oriented." Malcolm and Hulda Knowles (1959, p. 53) have devised a list of task-oriented behaviors which includes the following:

> *Initiating.* Suggesting new ideas or a changed way of looking at the group problem or goal, proposing new activities.
>
> *Information Seeking.* Asking for relevant facts or authoritative information.
>
> *Information Giving.* Providing relevant facts or authoritative information or relating personal experience pertinently to the group task.

*Opinion Giving.* Stating a pertinent belief or opinion about something the group is considering.

*Clarifying.* Probing for meaning and understanding, restating something the group is considering.

*Elaborating.* Building on a previous comment, enlarging on it, giving examples.

*Coordinating.* Showing or clarifying the relationships among various ideas, trying to pull ideas and suggestions together.

*Orienting.* Defining the progress of the discussion in terms of the group's goals, raising questions about the direction the discussion is taking.

*Testing.* Checking with the group to see if it is ready to make a decision or to take some action.

*Summarizing.* Reviewing the content of the past discussion.

The group's leader can engage in such behaviors, of course, but most of the group members also engage in task behaviors like these. Usually such behaviors will move the group closer to the completion of its task.

But group members also have personal needs. They don't always focus on the task itself; they use the group for socializing, ego-building, and in some cases aggression. Indeed, there is fairly strong evidence that a group will not be able to fulfill its task unless basic socio-emotional needs are being fulfilled for individuals.

When a group is functioning well, its members look out for one another's needs for status, acceptance, and friendship. Members will encourage each other, by being warm and friendly, by praising each other for their contributions, and by mediating and harmonizing conflicting viewpoints. Members will encourage participation by everyone (sometimes known as "gatekeeping") and will sometimes use humor to drain off tension or frustration. The group's goals can be met because everyone's social needs are also being met (Knowles and Knowles, 1959).

But groups don't always function harmoniously. Some individuals may interfere with the progress of a group by going off on a tangent, reciting irrelevant anecdotes, blocking concensus, or rejecting new ideas without giving them a fair hearing. Some individuals may use groups for aggressive behavior and may show hostility to other members of the group without apparent cause. Some may use the group to gain attention or recognition and may dominate the group with excessive talking, humor, or boisterous behavior. Sometimes members may try to dominate the group by making "power plays" or insisting on the adoption of their own point of view. Others may withdraw, act passive or indifferent, whisper, or doodle (Knowles and Knowles, 1959).

The college teacher who wishes to employ group methods in the classroom will need to become skilled at watching the behavior of individuals within a group. Groups will do well or poorly at performing their task depending on what goes on within the group. Every group needs a good group watcher.

## The Leader's Role

There has been much discussion of the role of the leader in groups. In some groups leaders play a crucial role; in others, such as groups that use leaderless or instrumented techniques, the leader is not even present.

A classic series of experiments on group leadership style was performed under the direction of Kurt Lewin during the 1930s. Lewin and his associates tested three types of leadership behavior: (1) authoritarian (policy determined by the leader), (2) democratic (all policies a matter of group discussion and decision, encouraged and assisted by the leader), and (3) laissez-faire (complete freedom for group or individual decision with a minimum of leader participation). Malcolm and Hulda Knowles report the following generalizations from the studies:

1. Authoritarian-led groups produced a greater quantity of work over a short period of time, but experienced more hostility, competition and aggression—especially scapegoating, more discontent beneath the surface, more dependence and less originality.

2. Democratically-led groups, slower in getting into production, were more strongly motivated, became increasingly productive with time and learning, experienced more friendliness and teamwork, praised one another more frequently and expressed greater satisfaction.

3. Laissez-faire groups did less work and poorer work than either of the others, spent more time in horse-play, talked more about what they should be doing, experienced more aggression than the democratic groups but less than the authoritarian, and expressed a preference for democratic leadership [1959, pp. 57-58].

It seems clear that for the college classroom some modification of a democratic leadership style is probably best, depending on the nature of the task.

When the college teacher assumes the role of group leader he or she takes on several responsibilities. First of all, the leader defines the learning task and sets the scene for a healthy learning environment. With some methods, such as the case study, the game, or a variety of instrumented techniques, the most important thing a teacher does is to select the method and the content of the material. Many college teachers, when they first begin to use group methods, complain that they feel guilty because they aren't doing anything. What they forget is that they spent a great deal of time in selecting the stimulus that started the group in motion. Sometimes a brief but clear statement of goals and ground rules can make all the difference with a group.

The leader also establishes a model for the behavior of group members. If the leader is argumentative, aggressive, and punishing, there is a good chance that group members will model that behavior in the group. If the leader wants the group to accept new ideas and consider all points of view, he or she will need to model that behavior.

The leader is the chief facilitator of communication in a group; he or she can review what is being said, reflect the feelings of group members, raise questions, point out disagreements, and note shared viewpoints. In general the leader tells the group what it is saying to itself and monitors its communication processes.

Finally, the leader participates in the group, sometimes as an observer and member, but very often, at least in the college classroom, as an "expert." It is always difficult to know exactly how much self-disclosure is appropriate for a leader, but there is a growing awareness that leaders are more effective when they participate authentically in a group rather than assume rigid roles. The college professor, by definition, often "knows" things that students do not. When the teacher is successful in keeping responsibility for the task on the group, he or she may feel free from time to time to join the group as an "expert-in-residence" to provide an informed viewpoint that the group may need and value. (Adapted from Tannenbaum, Weschler, and Massarik, 1970).

When groups are used in a college classroom, the professor (leader) usually needs to strike some balance between task functions and social functions. The group usually needs to achieve something, but not at the expense of the students' personal needs; likewise, students' needs must be met, but not at the expense of "learning" something. The teacher, therefore, is constantly in the middle as a facilitator of task and social functions. The role may be diagrammed as follows:

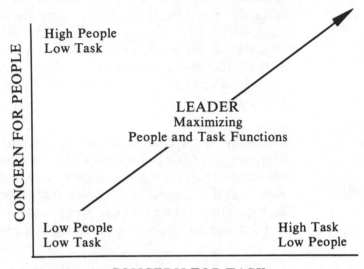

The effective group leader is able to maximize concern for task and social functions while turning the group into something greater than the sum of its participants.

## Learning in Groups

There is now a rather well-articulated set of principles about the kind of climate necessary for learning in groups. Many of the principles have grown out of studies of the interactions between client and therapist in psychiatric counseling. Others derive from the studies of interpersonal interactions in small groups, chiefly therapy groups and encounter groups. Those who have studied the client-therapist relationship and the relationships among persons in groups have noted well the

90

characteristics of the environment wherein change, growth, and learning seem most likely to take place. From these observations a set of principles have been drawn which describe how learning in groups seems to take place.

Many persons have attempted to describe the characteristics of environments which facilitate learning, most notably J. L. Moreno, Carl Rogers, Abraham Maslow, Roy Menninger, and Rollo May. There are many summaries of these characteristics available, but most include one or more of the following points:

1. *The learner must be actively involved.* In some way the learner must be caught up in the experience, cognitively, emotionally, and perhaps even physically. He must be doing something, not passively absorbing something. If possible, his whole being should be involved.

2. *That which is learned must touch the self.* At some significant level, what is being learned must touch the person. The learning must be personally relevant in some way so that the learner can feel that what is at hand is of significance to him.

3. *The person who facilitates the learning (teacher, leader, therapist) must be authentic and accepting.* The facilitator must communicate unconditional positive regard for the learner, empathy for his feelings, and acceptance of the learner as a person.

4. *The learning should involve a memorable insight.* The insight need not be dramatic, but some new understanding or clarification should be retained from the experience. The experience of growth should be memorable, and the learner should be able to describe how he now sees things differently.

5. *The facilitator assumes and draws upon the previous knowledge of the learner.* Instead of assuming that the learner knows little or nothing, the facilitator draws

upon the existing knowledge of the learner and helps
to forge new insights based on what he already knows.

6. *Learning involves interpersonal relations.* Learning
is a function of interpersonal relations; it takes place
in the presence of persons and is mediated by persons.
As such it is intensely personal.

The six principles outlined above are well summarized
in the following paragraphs from a lecture given by
Carl Rogers at Harvard:

> When I have been able to transform a group—and
> here I mean all the members of a group, myself
> included—into a community of *learners,* then the
> excitement has been almost beyond belief. To free
> curiosity; to open everything to questioning and explora-
> tion; to recognize that everything is in process of
> change—here is an experience I can never forget. I
> cannot always achieve it in groups with which I am
> associated but when it is partially or largely achieved
> then it becomes a never-to-be-forgotten group experience.
> Out of such a context arise true students, real learners,
> creative scientists and scholars and practitioners, the
> kind of individuals who can live in a delicate but
> ever-changing balance between what is presently known
> and the flowing, moving, altering, problems and facts
> of the future. . . . We know . . . that the initiation of
> such learning rests not upon the teaching skills of the
> leader, not upon his scholarly knowledge of the field,
> not upon his curricular planning, not upon his use
> of audio-visual aids, not upon the programmed learning
> he utilizes, not upon his lectures and presentations,
> not upon an abundance of books, though each of
> these might at one time or another be utilized as an
> important resource. No, the facilitation of significant
> learning rests upon certain attitudinal qualities which
> exist in the personal *relationship* between the
> facilitator and the learner [Rogers, 1966].

## Implications for Teaching

There are, of course, an endless number of group methods. Many are designed for examining or cultivating group processes in themselves rather than for teaching something specific about a subject. The college teacher who wishes to employ a group technique as a teaching strategy needs to adapt the method to suit a particular educational goal. The college teacher must be on the alert for various methods that can be reworked to fit a particular pedagogical need. The great danger in suggesting "methods that work" is that people tend to take them over and apply them unaltered in a different situation, one which may doom them to failure from the start. The college teacher who uses group methods should get the feeling of how groups work and then invent or adapt methods that will aid in attaining a desired goal.

Instead of reviewing all the types of methods and techniques that are available, I have compiled a list of 10 types of group processes that are frequently used in college classrooms. The examples will "work" only if adapted to your particular interests and needs.

1. *Get-acquainted activities.* Sometimes people in a class need to get acquainted with each other before they can engage in any significant discussion of a subject, particularly if opinions, attitudes, and beliefs are involved. If the class is large, it sometimes helps to get acquainted with at least a few individuals. There are several ways to get acquainted and the general principle involves giving people an excuse to talk about themselves. One way is to give students a sheet of unfinished statements such as:

I'm best at . . .

I'm not very good at . . .

Basically, I'm the kind of person that . . .

I need to . . .

Students can get together in pairs or small groups to discuss their answers. Another list might include words that summarize values, for example:

| | |
|---|---|
| freedom | pleasure |
| order | accomplishment |
| cleanliness | excitement |
| compassion | recognition |
| self-respect | security |

Students are asked to rank order the list and discuss with a partner or small group the reasons for the ordering. Still another device asks students to draw the floor plan of the house where they grew up. They share it with a partner or a small group and in the process reveal a lot about "where they are coming from."

2. *Working in pairs.* Many teachers say they can't use groups because their class is held in a large lecture hall with fixed seating. But a group, as we have noted above, can be composed of two people. This might be the person seated directly beside, in front of, or behind a student. There is no rule that says that students have to *sit* in the chairs, so it may be useful to have students go find a partner and talk "beer-party style" standing around for a few minutes. Almost anything can be taught with partners. The biological and physical sciences have used lab partners for years. We are now learning that music students of approximately equal ability work well in pairs. Students in composition courses work well in tandem as critics, as do budding philosophers in criticizing the logic of arguments and position papers. It is usually easy to share personal opinions and beliefs with just one other individual.

3. *Discussion starters.* Many teachers find it difficult
to get discussions started. They complain that students
"just sit there." One classic discussion starter is the
agree/disagree list. Students are asked to respond to
a list of 5 or 10 statements by marking them either
"agree" or "disagree." When students begin to share
their marking of the statements, a lively discussion
usually ensues. Another useful technique is to use a brief
questionnaire that asks each student to state a position
on a controversial issue. One questionnaire on the topic
of abortion included the following questions:

> Do you think that every woman should have the
> right to abortion without qualification?
>
> Should the father be involved in decisions about
> abortion?
>
> At what point do you believe that human life
> begins?
>
> In what circumstances, if any, are you most likely
> to object to abortion?

Students complete the questionnaires quickly, sign their
names, and pass the forms in to the instructor. The
instructor guides the discussion by calling on people
to elaborate their position: "Suzie, I see that you've
answered the first question in the negative." "John,
I note that you disagree with Suzie." "Jane, your answer
to question three intrigues me; can you tell us more?"
The structure can be dropped gradually as the discussion
takes shape.

4. *Participants/Observers.* Some people tend to dominate
a discussion; others seem to hang back. That pattern
can be broken up by designating certain students as
participants on some days and making them observers
on other days. By assigning specific roles to observers—
for example, having them monitor the behavior of an
individual or "keep score" on the behavior of the group—
everyone gets involved and in some sense participates.

This is also a good device for breaking a large group into a manageable size for a discussion.

5. *Competitive groups.* Most college students enjoy competitive team activities, and teams can be used in many disciplines. The object is to pose a task—such as completing a chemical analysis, gathering certain kinds of flora, or mastering a physical skill—that the group can work on together. Competitive teams actually have to turn into internally cooperative teams, and if used properly they can function in such a way as to have the brightest or most skilled work hard to aid those who need help most. An entire group will often focus on helping the weakest link if that link is crucial to the success of the team. I once observed a group of seven in an intermediate swimming class focus its entire attention on helping one member of the group develop an adequate kick turn.

6. *Cooperative groups.* Instead of setting competition as a goal, the instructor can ask the group to complete a project which *requires* cooperation. Almost any project will work when the group has to produce a product. Groups of students can work cooperatively on producing a short film or videotape, painting a picture, working out a teaching unit for an elementary science curriculum, or developing and marketing a product as a small business. Students often work well as cooperative teams in conducting survey research (public opinion polls) in the social sciences. A natural division of labor can be worked out according to the special skills or competencies of individual members of the group.

7. *Instruments.* Sometimes all a group needs is a good initial stimulus. Instruments may pose a problem, set the scene for a discussion, or ask the group to complete certain operations. Newspaper, magazine, and journal articles, if carefully chosen, can serve as good instruments, as can riddles and puzzles. In management training, "in-basket" items are often used to simulate

96

real problems that may cross a manager's desk; students enjoy comparing their responses in small groups. Some instruments provide enough instructions for a leaderless group to function for an entire class period. If you need to miss a class, send an instrument.

8. *Cases.* The case method has been developed and refined to a high level of sophistication in the teaching of management and organizational operations. A case usually consists of several pages of background material on an organizational, communication, or personnel problem in the context of a specific institution. The case usually breaks off in the middle with instructions such as: "You are the manager (supervisor); what would you do?" Students in the group generate options and argue the merits of various solutions. Some cases are progressive; that is, the discussion can be stopped and new material can be introduced, facts and figures which might change the course of the discussion. Cases may be focused on the problems of individuals as well as organizations. Videotaped or filmed studies of personality problems or interpersonal conflicts may be the subjects of case studies used in courses in psychology, social work, or counseling.

9. *Role-playing.* Students may be asked to act out a particular problem or situation as a stimulus to further discussion. In effective role-playing, the roles are clearly defined, usually through a thumbnail sketch of a character or situation provided in writing. Sometimes the initial dialogue will be established to get the "actors" into their parts. Role-playing works well where professional skills are being learned, where students are being socialized into the role behavior of doctor, attorney, pastor, or counselor. Videotape playbacks (instant replays) are often useful in conjunction with role-playing. A helpful twist involves asking persons in adversary roles to switch places and play the role of the person they have been opposing.

10. *Games*. People have always played games, some more serious than others. Serious games have been the object of study for some time and "game theory," a branch of mathematics, dates back to the 1920s with the work of Borel and to the 1940s with the work of Von Neuman and Morgenstern. Today game theorists classify games as "zero-sum," "cooperative," "noncooperative," "n-person," and "group-decision making." In general, games involve two or more persons, specific information, rules, opposing interests or conflict, finite materials or settings, and goals or conclusions. There are several classic games used in teaching at the college level. The American Management Association's "Top Management Decision Simulation" was developed in 1957 and is widely used in business courses. "Starpower," a game about social status and power, is used in sociology and political science. "Inter-nation Simulation" is used in international relations, as is "Bafa-Bafa," to teach about "culture shock." Psychology classes use "Personalysis" to help students understand their own personality. And to teach ecology a professor can draw on "Pollution," "Smog," or "Dirty Water."*

Among the 10 types of group processes listed above are to be found techniques which most college teachers can adapt to achieve some academically respectable educational changes in opinions, attitudes, and values. It is likely, however, that if such changes are to take place at all, it will be through an interpersonal exchange in a small group. Above all, groups are fun; they are likely to make what has often been a grim experience a little more enjoyable for students and for the teacher, too.

*A basic reference, with brief descriptions of appropriate games for various fields, is David W. Zuckerman and Robert E. Horn's *The Guide to Simulation Games for Education and Training* (Information Resources, Inc.; 1675 Massachusetts Avenue; Cambridge, Massachusetts 02138). If you don't find what you need among the over 400 games listed, make up your own.

# References

Bales, Robert F. *Interaction Process Analysis: A Method for the Study of Small Groups.* Cambridge, Mass.: Addison-Wesley, 1950.

Barbour, Alton, and Alvin A. Goldberg. *Interpersonal Communication: Teaching Strategies and Resources.* New York: Speech Communication Association, 1974.

Berelson, Bernard, and Gary A. Steiner. *Human Behavior: An Inventory of Scientific Findings.* New York: Harcourt, Brace & World, 1964.

Burton, Arthur. *Encounter.* San Francisco: Jossey-Bass, 1969.

Gibbard, Graham S., John J. Hartman, and Richard D. Mann. *Analysis of Groups.* San Francisco: Jossey-Bass, 1974.

Knowles, Malcolm, and Hulda Knowles. *Introduction to Group Dynamics.* New York: Association Press, 1959.

Lewin, Kurt. "Forces Behind Food Habits and Methods of Change." *Bulletin of The National Research Council,* 108 (1943): 35-65.

Lieberman, Morton A., Irvin D. Yalom, and Matthew B. Miles. *Encounter Groups: First Facts.* New York: Basic Books, 1973.

Lorge, Irving, et al. "A Survey of the Studies Contrasting the Quality of Group Performance and Individual Performance, 1920-1957." *Psychological Bulletin,* 55 (1958): 337-372.

Phillips, Gerald M. *Communication and the Small Group.* New York: The Bobbs-Merrill Co., 1973.

Rogers, Carl. *On Encounter Groups.* New York: Harper & Row, 1970.

Rogers, Carl. "The Interpersonal Relationship in the Facilitation of Learning." Lecture given at Harvard University, April 12, 1966.

Tannenbaum, Robert, Irving R. Weschler, and Fred Massarik. "The Role of The Trainer." In Robert T. Golembiewski and Arthur Blumberg, *Sensitivity Training And The Laboratory Approach.* Itasca, Ill.: F. E. Peacock, Publishers, 1970.

Verny, Thomas R. *Inside Groups.* New York: McGraw-Hill, 1974.

Wheeler, Ladd. *Interpersonal Influence.* Boston: Allyn Bacon, 1970.

# Choosing and Using
# A Teaching Strategy

In the preface to Daniel Bell's *The Reforming of General Education* (Garden City, N.Y.: Doubleday & Co., 1968) there is recounted a delightful folk tale about a rabbi who has agreed to adjudicate a controversy between two women. The rabbi listens patiently to the first woman's case, and when she is finished, he nods his head thoughtfully and says, "You are absolutely right!" The rabbi's wife reminds him that he ought to hear the other side of the controversy as well. When the second woman has presented her case, the rabbi nods thoughtfully and says, "You are absolutely right!" His wife is dismayed. "Dear rabbi," she says, "they can't both be right." The rabbi turns to his wife, nods thoughtfully, and says, "You are absolutely right!" [p. xxi].

In reading books or listening to discussions about college teaching, it is easy to fall into the trap which ensnared the rabbi: The theory with the greatest "truth" seems to be the one which was last presented. At certain times, given certain assumptions and goals, the argument of the behaviorists carries the day. Under other conditions the viewpoint of cognitive psychologists makes more sense. For some, learning is primarily inquiry. Others find the case for using group processes to be convincing. It is difficult to know who is right and which strategy to choose.

The differences between the various strategies are real and significant. The importance of these divergencies should not be overlooked, and efforts to probe the underlying assumptions of conflicting theories about how people learn should be pursued vigorously. The advocates of different strategies are not "all saying the same thing."

For example, beneath each of the strategies are some assumptions about human motivation. The behaviorist recognizes the importance of external reinforcement in producing motivation. Although the properties of a reinforcer are relative to the learner's own peculiar sense of what is pleasant, motivation, for the behaviorist, is essentially "out there." It is cast in the event which follows a particular behavior. Thus, the teacher who uses behavioral learning theory and a systems approach to instruction will direct a great deal of attention to arranging external reinforcers to insure that the learner is motivated. The teacher who uses an inquiry strategy, on the other hand, assumes that the process of problem-solving is itself motivating. This teacher believes that human beings, by their very nature, want answers, that motivation comes naturally, through the innate curiosity of being human, and that inquiry needs no external reward. The teacher who employs group processes takes a still different view of motivation. In this case, motivation is sparked by the social interaction that takes place in groups. People, being basically social in nature, are motivated when given the opportunity to learn by interacting with others.

Similarly, each strategy seems to imply a slightly different emphasis on what is important in teaching. The behaviorist wants to stress skills. Cognitive psychologists stress information. Those who use an inquiry strategy stress the reasoning process, while those who use groups are more cognizant of the affective dimensions of learning. The differences among the four strategies are significant.

## Some Similarities

Yet the striking aspect of the principles and theories presented in the four teaching strategies is not their dissimilarity, but rather their underlying continuity. It is possible, by stepping back from the various strategies, to extract from them some recurrent themes.

For example, no matter what strategy you choose, teaching is complex. Everything matters. The behaviorist must work carefully to design an instructional system where the contingencies of reinforcement are arranged precisely to move the learner step by step to desired goals. The skilled lecturer does not just stand up and talk.

Similarly, all of the strategies require clear objectives— if not stated in precise behaviorial terms, then at least well conceived in the teacher's mind. Each strategy requires that the teacher have a precise sense of what is being undertaken, why it is being undertaken, and what the outcomes will be.

Furthermore, all of the strategies require precision in the communication process. Whether communication takes place through computer-assisted instruction, a lecture, or a small group, the exchange must be precise and clear. A great deal of teaching obviously falters on poor communication.

Likewise, all of the strategies require some knowledge of "where the student is." The teacher cannot afford to dwell in blissful ignorance with regard to what the student already knows, what is relevant to the student, and what the student is feeling during the learning process.

## Which Strategy Is Best?

Given these differences and similarities among the strategies, how does the thoughtful teacher decide which strategy is best? There are several ways.

First, the teacher may, on the basis of educational philosophy and personal preference, choose the strategy that seems to fit his or her personal needs. Some teachers have an incredible talent for lecturing. (Most do not, I would hasten to add.) For the teacher who lectures well, lecturing—the informed transmission of information outlined as Teaching Strategy 2—is a suitable mode. It would be a terrible waste to have a brilliant lecturer suddenly decide to use only programmed instruction or instrumented group processes. Similarly, a person who just can't keep from talking may never learn to use an inquiry strategy. Some people are excellent facilitators of groups; what a pity for them to long to be renowned lecturers. Each teacher must find those strategies with which he or she feels comfortable. After some adventurous exploration of new strategies, a teacher may wish to select one that best suits his or her philosophy and talents and use it consistently.

Second, the teacher may wish to choose a strategy that best suits the needs of the students. If we have learned anything about teaching and learning in the last 25 years it is that people learn in different ways. For some students a systems approach will be best. In other settings, particularly with adults, groups will work best. The most helpful criterion may not be what suits the teacher best, but rather what suits the students best.

Third, the teacher may want to choose a strategy that best fits the goals of the course or lesson. As mentioned above, each strategy seems to be useful in achieving slightly different goals. If the desired outcome is change in opinions, attitudes, and beliefs, a programmed text is probably a bad choice. If the teacher wishes to convey some background information to introduce a subject, a group technique would not be as effective as a lecture.

Some teachers will become masters of one strategy, others will draw eclectically from all four. Some, for the sake of variety, will use one approach one day and another approach on another day. Recall the question that was posed in our discussion of research on college teaching: Under what conditions do what students learn what things? In choosing a teaching strategy, the college teacher might ask: What students will learn what things if I use this strategy?

## Above All, Choose Some Strategy

However the decision is made, the important thing is that some choice of teaching strategy *must* take place. If there is one single point to be made by this book, it is this: Teaching is not talking and learning is not listening! The effective teacher is one who has considered carefully the literature on how people learn. Unless a teacher's approach to instruction is informed by some underlying concept of how people learn, it is unlikely that much actual learning will take place. Unless the teacher has reflected seriously on what the outcomes of a particular course, unit, or lesson should be, there is little chance that either the teacher or student will attain these outcomes. Unless the teacher "knows what he is doing" in the deepest sense of that phrase, his most dedicated efforts will turn out to be sound and fury signifying nothing. There are accidents of course;

some teachers teach and some students learn without much thought being given to the process by either one. Some teachers *are* born—a very small percentage— but the rest of us have to work fairly hard at the task. How ironic that academicians, supposedly dedicated to the use of rational processes in human affairs, would leave to chance their own activity in the classroom. There are accidentally good teachers; but most of us, if we don't establish the process by reason, will just have bad accidents. Having a teaching strategy, for most teachers, can make all the difference.

## Evaluating Teaching

There is an enormous amount of attention being directed toward the evaluation of teaching today. Almost every college and university has some formal or informal method of evaluating teaching. Teachers are involved in peer reviews of colleagues, administrators are asked to make judgments about teachers with regard to promotion and tenure, and students, as the consumers of teaching, are insinuating themselves into the evaluation process. What is troublesome is that so much of the activity is so superficial.

I have reviewed the evaluation instruments of some 50 programs, departments, and colleges. They follow an almost identical pattern. Most involve questionnaires which ask students, usually at the end of the course, to respond to selected items, supposedly designed to evaluate the teacher's classroom performance. The questionnaires may provide for a simple "yes" or "no" check or may use a Likert-type scale with responses such as "agree," "strongly agree" or "always," "sometimes," "never." As might be anticipated, most students check something in the middle—over a whole term it's hard to say that a professor "always" or "never" does anything—and the overall rating turns out to be a mixed bag, damning the instructor with faint praise.

More disturbing is the nature of the items. A sample of items selected from various evaluation instruments, many from prestigious colleges and universities, appears below:

> Held my attention and interest.
> Emphasized principles and generalizations.
> Was responsive to students' comments and questions.
> Helped broaden my interests.
> Made good use of examples and illustrations.
> Knew the subject matter.
> Gave me new viewpoints and appreciations.
> Was clear and understandable in giving explanations.
> Was helpful to individual students.
> Integrated the material into a coherent whole.
> Discussed recent developments in the field.
> Was well prepared.
> Was friendly toward students.
> Gave examinations that were clear and fair.

Most of the items which appear in this list do little to discriminate between effective and ineffective teaching. Rather, the items represent behaviors and attitudes which we ought to take for granted as minimal requirements for every college teacher. Before a teacher enters the classroom, students and colleagues ought to be able to *assume* that a teacher has thoroughly mastered the subject. We ought to *assume* that the teacher cares about the subject and is passionately involved in its presentation. We ought to *assume* that a teacher has warm personal regard for students, and that questions will be answered directly and without embarrassment to the student. We should *assume* that the examination process is clear and fair and that exams cover the material presented in the course. There is something inane about asking students such questions on evaluation forms, and it is disheartening to think that the people who use such forms really think they are evaluating *teaching*. Such forms, it seems to me, may be useful in evaluating whether the teacher should be allowed to step into the classroom, but some very ineffective teachers ought to be able to score well on questionnaires like these. That is to say, most questionnaires used to evaluate teaching don't discriminate between good and poor teaching at all.

Teaching, as we have noted, is a fairly complex process. It involves the use of a clear and identifiable teaching strategy, which in turn involves a theoretical framework for conceptualizing how people learn. Effective teaching involves far more than knowing one's subject, being a nice person, and answering questions politely. Effective teaching emerges from the skillful employment of a particular strategy to achieve a specific goal. The real evaluation of effective teaching *begins* where most pat evaluations of teaching *end*. The essential question is this: Does the teacher employ a teaching strategy with skill and some finesse? In evaluating a college teacher what we want to know is whether the instructor is skillful, artful, adroit, and subtle in employing a strategy that results in *learning,* learning that is observable, measurable, self-evident, and obvious to all, learning that one wants to stand up and applaud and cheer, because it has emerged with such grace and elegance. When a teaching strategy really works, we should want to stand back and (with nod and a grin) say, "How neat!"

The evaluation of teaching, therefore, must take place under the guidance of some people who know something about *teaching.* Colleagues may know something about teaching, but not necessarily. Students may also know something about teaching, but not necessarily. It is not always possible to evaluate a doctor simply by being the patient. What is called for is a team of students and colleagues who have a common frame of reference and some sense about the nature of a teacher's professional competence. In the evaluation of college teaching we must begin to use as evaluators people who have taken the trouble to find out what teaching and learning is really all about and who are willing to probe the teaching process deeply enough to discover whether the teacher who is being evaluated has any ability in employing a teaching strategy. The evaluation probably can't be done with a form or check list. If we really want to evaluate teaching we will need to watch teachers teach. To be effective an evaluation visit should result in some straight talk and probing questions, whereby the teacher being evaluated is drawn into a process of self-evaluation. The overriding consideration for the observers should be: Does the teacher employ a strategy for achieving identifiable goals and employ an approach to instruction that grows out of a theoretical framework for conceptualizing learning?

## Faculty Development

As is the case with faculty evaluation, many of the efforts to improve teaching, known widely today as "faculty development" programs, are superficial and without much impact. Teaching behavior will not change rapidly or without great effort; the "talking tradition" is deeply imbedded in the subculture of the American professorate. There is a great need for programs designed to improve teaching competence among professors. The concept of "faculty development" is valid; but unfortunately, much that is done is so superficial that little change in teaching behavior results.

Faculty development programs take on several forms. Often the focus is exhortation. The faculty gathers to hear a speech on teaching improvement, the need for better classroom instruction, perhaps even the report of a national study citing the need for renewed emphasis on teaching. Everyone agrees that teaching (translate "other teachers' teaching") needs to be improved and that something needs to be done. The listeners gain some inspiration from the speech and feel better—teachers

can always use some inspiration because teaching is
a tough task—but when they return to the classroom,
they realize they haven't learned what to do to change
their teaching.

Other faculty development programs focus on institutional impediments to teaching, the so-called reward
structure. If only (so it is said) we could get administrators
to evaluate the importance of teaching and reward
teaching excellence in decisions about promotion and
tenure, then somehow—the somehow is never explained—
the general level of teaching will improve. Teaching is
pitted against research. Class size and teaching loads
are attacked as unreasonable and "committee overload"
is identified as a chief contributor to the decline of
teaching quality. To right these wrongs, a committee
is formed to address the conditions of employment that
detract from teaching. The assumption behind all this
activity is that lack of time is the chief barrier to effective teaching. No one stops to think that some teachers,
given all the time in the world, still wouldn't know
what to do to improve their teaching.

Other faculty development programs focus on the in-
terior, personal impediments to change. A week-end,
let-it-all-hang-out t-group is offered where colleagues
can examine their hang-ups about themselves, their
attitudes about students, their feelings about the profession, the university, their country, and the human
condition generally. Such sessions can be revealing, and
often are, but on Monday morning a renewed and liberated
self returns to the classroom and finds, alas, the same
dog-eared lecture notes and the same tired students,
not at all liberated, but enslaved by their note-taking,
a tradition that no one seems to know how to break.

While some of the issues discussed in "traditional"
faculty development programs may serve as a necessary
prolegomena to serious discussion of teaching, faculty
"development" will not take place unless, at some point,

110

faculty members are engaged in serious confrontation of the need for a teaching strategy. Unless we talk about how people learn and the strategies and techniques that can be used in the classroom to maximize learning, the noble objectives we all share for the improvement of teaching will never be reached. Furthermore, we can't just talk about teaching strategies; we need to *use* them. The leaders of faculty development workshops must involve people in using computer-assisted instruction, in leading an inquiry-discussion, or in employing role-playing or psychodrama. Teachers must experience what it is like to be taught when a teaching strategy is used, and they must experience first-hand what happens when they employ a teaching strategy. Like most classrooms, most faculty development workshops could profit from less talk and more action.

Finally, for teaching behavior to change, the conversation about teaching strategies needs to get very specific. Teaching is a subject that invites abstract generalizations. The real issue is: What did you do in the classroom on that hour and why did you do it? Such discussion takes place best not in large groups or conferences but in a teacher-mentor relationship, where two people who trust each other can talk seriously about their successes and failures in the classroom. Just as every psychiatrist is encouraged to have his own psychiatrist, every teacher ought to have a master-teacher, a colleague-mentor, who can say, "Have you tried this?" "Would this be a good strategy for that?" "If that failed, what about this?" "Were you aware that you were doing that?" The mentor becomes a sounding board for new ideas, a person who looks over the shoulder, a source of encouragement and support. Faculty development takes place best when every teacher realizes that he or she has something to gain from and offer to another colleague.

Thomas Jefferson spoke of an aristocracy of merit growing out of a democracy of opportunity. If ever there was a democracy of opportunity, it is in the field of college teaching. Although there are some institutional impediments to the improvement of college teaching, most of the so-called obstacles are rationalizations. There is probably no profession where one can fail quietly, without condemnation, as easily as in college teaching; on the other hand, there is probably no profession where one finds fewer impediments to being truly successful. I have presented in some detail in this book four teaching strategies which can be used in the college classroom. Surely, some of the strategies will work for you. Use them, modify and perfect them, and become the great teacher you can become.

# A Bibliographic Essay:
# Books About
# College Teaching

It is instructive to see what has been written about a particular field of endeavor. Those who write about a subject shape the subject through the questions they ask, the priority they give to the study of particular aspects of the subject, and the information they regard as important in understanding the subject. By examining what has been written about a field it is possible to discern trends in what has been said and, more important perhaps, what has been left unsaid or treated superficially. It is particularly instructive to see what has been written—and not been written—about college teaching.

My purpose in writing this bibliographic essay has been to categorize the books on college teaching by type, to suggest books that are helpful in understanding particular things about college teaching, and to draw some conclusions about what this writing about college teaching has to say about the way professors regard the task of teaching. In doing so, I have not listed every book that has ever been written about college teaching, but rather, I have tried to select representative types from the categories I have developed. I have limited the study to books and have focused on current works.

Those who are interested in searching for books on college teaching soon find that there is no one, central bibliographical source. There are, however, several bibliographies, each of which contributes helpful information about important works. It is interesting to note that the index of *Books in Print* for 1974 lists only 19 books under the subject heading "College Teaching." There are not many current books, and some of the more helpful volumes are out of print and are only to be found in the stacks of libraries with sizable collections. The most comprehensive bibliography of the literature on college teaching is one developed by Walter Eells entitled *College Teachers and College Teaching* (Atlanta: Southern Regional Education Board, 1957). It has been updated with three supplements, two by Walter Eells in 1959 and 1962 and one by Maurice L. Litton and W. Hugh Stickler in 1967. This is the best bibliographic source, but it is difficult to use, ironically, because it includes such a vast collection of listings, particularly of periodical literature. Also helpful are Lewis Mayhew's annual listings of books on higher education and a recent bibliography on higher education prepared by Paul Dressel and Sally Pratt entitled *The World of Higher Education* (San Francisco: Jossey-Bass, 1971). When these bibliographies have been exhausted, the search must turn to the Library of Congress listings under the subject category "College Teaching" or to listings in various academic disciplines under the subheading "Study and Teaching."

## Studies Sponsored by Professional Associations

College teaching has been a topic of continuing concern to various higher education professional associations, and many of the books on college teaching have been sponsored in one way or another by such associations. The American Council on Education has sponsored three publications on college teaching. The earliest is a modest work which explores the role of graduate teaching assistants. It is authored by Vincent Nowlis, Kenneth E. Clark, and Miriam Rock and is entitled *The Graduate*

*Student as Teacher* (Washington: American Council on Education, 1968). Better known is Calvin Lee's edited volume, *Improving College Teaching* (Washington: American Council on Education, 1966). This work contains the background papers for participants in the 49th Annual Meeting of the American Council. Essays by major figures range over a wide range of topics from "Conflicting Academic Loyalties" to "Who Teaches the Teachers?" A more helpful work is the book edited by William H. Morris entitled *Effective College Teaching: The Quest for Relevance* (Washington: American Council on Education, 1970). Sponsored by the Joint Committee on College Teaching as a cooperative project of several major higher education professional associations, it is directed toward the peculiar problems of instruction in various subject fields.

Another general study was conducted by the American Association of Colleges for Teacher Education (AACTE) and resulted in a volume entitled *Improvement of Instruction in Higher Education* (Washington: American Association of Colleges for Teacher Education, 1962). More helpful is the AACTE publication entitled *Conceptual Models in Teacher Education,* edited by John Verdan, Jr. (Washington: American Association of Colleges for Teacher Education, 1967). This is one of the most worthwhile theoretical discussions of teaching ever compiled. Although it is directed primarily toward teacher education, it is useful for college teachers generally. A third AACTE publication, *College Teachers Look At College Teaching* (Washington: American Association of Colleges for Teacher Education, 1965), is a report of two seminars sponsored by the association to identify elements of good college teaching. Although much of the volume deals with participants' contributions to and evaluation of the seminar, there are selections dealing with research on successful college teaching and factors that contribute to or hinder outstanding teaching performances.

The most recent and most comprehensive study of college teaching was that conducted jointly by the Association

115

of American Colleges and the American Association
of University Professors. Under the direction of Kenneth
Eble the study resulted in the publication of two monographs, *The Recognition and Evaluation of Teaching*
and *Career Development of the Effective College Teacher*
(Washington: American Association of University Professors and Association of American Colleges, 1970 and
1971 respectively), and a major book by Kenneth Eble,
*Professors as Teachers* (San Francisco: Jossey-Bass,
1972). Eble's volume grew out of extensive visits to
college and university campuses across the nation and
includes important observations about how teaching is,
in fact, carried out in the typical college classroom and
how teachers are trained, evaluated, and rewarded. It
was not within the scope of the study to provide concrete advice about the techniques and processes of effective
teaching, but Eble's book is perhaps the most important
recent volume on college teaching, and its recommendations
are as much directed toward administrators as teachers.

The continuing interest of the professional associations
in college teaching (with the notable omission of any
major work by the Carnegie Commission) suggests that
those in positions of influence shaping national policy
share a continuing concern for the improvement of
instruction in institutions of higher education. Unfortunately, the concern often grows out of a vague
uneasiness that "all is not well" and a feeling that
"something should be done," but becomes expressed in
forms that analyze the context in which teaching is
done without penetrating the teaching-learning process
itself. Helpful as such studies are, they do little *in
themselves* to improve instruction or provide the classroom teacher with tools, techniques, concepts, theories,
or strategies which are directly applicable to classroom
teaching.

116

The concern of the professional associations for the improvement of college teaching has been echoed in a number of books which might be classified as exhortations to better teaching. Typical of such books is C. E. Rothwell and associates' *The Importance of Teaching: A Memorandum to the New College Teacher* (New Haven: The Hazen Foundation, 1968). Growing out of the Hazen Foundation's interest in its fellowship program for college teachers, this work is very general and urges young teachers to nurture good teaching but does not explore what good teaching really is. Similar exhortations may be found in Joseph Justman and Walter H. Mais's *College Teaching: Its Practice and Its Potential* (New York: Harper and Brothers, 1956), in Ordway Tead's *College Teaching and College Learning: A Plea for Improvement* (New Haven: Yale University Press, 1949), and in Earl V. Pulias and Aileene Lockhart's *Toward Excellence in Teaching* (Dubuque, Iowa: Wm. C. Brown, 1963). Perhaps the best and most useful of the exhortations to better teaching is the collection of reprints of articles by well-known scholars which appears in Ohmer Milton and Edward Joseph Shoben, Jr.'s *Learning and the Professors* (Athens: Ohio University Press, 1968).

Moving persons to improvement and change—especially professors—often involves exhortation. It is important to be reminded from time to time that the quality of college teaching can and must be improved, but such volumes are of limited value unless accompanied by companion works which discuss in some depth the nature of effective teaching and the concrete steps that can be taken by college teachers to improve classroom instruction.

There are several general books on college teaching. Such books usually follow a familiar format, beginning with general chapters about higher education, the pressing issues of the day, the history of higher education in America, and the goals of classroom instruction. They usually have a few chapters on various techniques of instruction, a chapter on evaluation, and (perhaps) a chapter on motivation or how students learn. They have set the pattern for the "typical" book on college teaching.

Some of these books have been more helpful than others and some have even become "classics" in the field. By far the most helpful of these general books for the classroom teacher is Russell Cooper's *The Two Ends of the Log: Learning And Teaching In Today's College* (Minneapolis: University of Minnesota Press, 1958). This book contains chapters by outstanding scholars, such as Nevitt Sanford's "The Professor Looks at the Student," Wilbert McKeachie's "How Do Students Learn?" and Ralph Tyler's "The Evaluation of Teaching." In the last half of the book individual chapters are devoted to various teaching techniques such as role-playing, the case method, discussion, etc. In spite of the book's being 15 years old, it is still a helpful general volume for the college teacher.

Another classic is Claude Buxton's *College Teaching: A Psychologist's View* (New York: Harcourt, Brace and Co., 1956). One would expect to find, given the title of the volume, an interpretation of learning theory for college teachers; but, unfortunately, Buxton speaks more as a professor than as a psychologist, and does not make the anticipated synthesis. Also in the category of classic is Gilbert Highet's *The Art of Teaching* (New York: Knopf, 1950). Highet's book continues to confound those who seek to establish teaching as a "science" or a "technology" as opposed to an art.

118

Other books which follow the format of general books on college teaching are James G. Umstattd's *College Teaching: Background, Theory and Practice* (Washington: University Press of Washington, 1964), Henry C. Herge's *The College Teacher* (New York: Center for Applied Research in Education, 1965), James Brown and James W. Thornton, Jr.'s *College Teaching: Perspectives and Guidelines* (New York: McGraw-Hill, 1963), Brown and Thornton's newer book, *College Teaching: A Systematic Approach* (New York: McGraw-Hill, 1971), and Hermin Estrin and Delmer Goode's *College and University Teaching* (Dubuque, Iowa: Wm. C. Brown Co., 1964). Ohmer Milton's recent book, *Alternatives to the Traditional* (San Francisco: Jossey-Bass, 1973), although similar to these general books, attempts to go beyond them by confronting the questions: How do professors teach? How do students learn? Milton sets forth research evidence on learning in an attempt to challenge traditional teaching practices. Though his concern for "new approaches" leads him away from classroom teaching to discussions of curricular innovations, Milton's is a helpful and stimulating volume.

The general books provide important insights and the distilled wisdom of thoughtful scholars, but like the works sponsored by professional associations, they fail too often to offer help for the classroom teacher. They are excellent books, as far as they go, but they speak too seldom of what is actually taking place when a teacher is "teaching" and a student is "learning." One must raise the question after reviewing these general works: Why are college professors reluctant to develop theoretical frameworks for examining in depth the nature of the teaching-learning process?

There are a few practical handbooks on college teaching and books that discuss "methods" such as the lecture method, discussion method, etc. The best known of these is *Teaching Tips* by Wilbert McKeachie (Ann Arbor, Mich.: The George Wahr Publishing Co., 1965). McKeachie's book, subtitled *A Guide-Book for the Beginning College Teacher,* is very practical and includes chapters on "Meeting a Class for the First Time," "Getting Students into Seats," "The ABC's of Assigning Grades," and "Morale, Discipline and Order." Many new teachers have found the book helpful in providing guidance in meeting practical problems. Another helpful handbook, which comes from abroad, is Ruth Beard's *Teaching and Learning in Higher Education* (Harmondsworth, Middlesex, England: Penguin, 1970). It discusses the strengths and weaknesses of various methods of instruction and adds an international perspective to the literature.

Two of the more helpful books on "methods" are surveys of teaching practice. They are J. G. Umstattd's *Teaching Procedures: Used in Twenty-Eight Midwestern and South-western Colleges and Universities* (Austin, Tex.: The University Co-operative Society, 1954) and Delmer M. Goode's *Seventy-Two College Teaching Procedures* (Corvallis: Oregon State University Press, 1966).

Most college teachers have an inbred aversion to discussing "methods" and to many the term connotes the superficiality associated with the less effective (and now hopefully extinct) teacher training "methods" courses. The aversion, apart from the stereotype, is not altogether unwarranted. While it may be helpful to categorize the various approaches to teaching (lecture, discussion, laboratory, field trip, etc.), such so-called "methods" are hardly homogeneous and distinct approaches to instruction. One can doubtless learn (or not learn) through a variety of these "methods," and whether the student does so or not probably depends on a host of factors more important than the particular "method" used. To discuss college teaching in terms of various "methods" is no longer very helpful.

## Books on Theories of Learning

From time to time college teachers bent on improving their instruction have turned to psychologists for information about how people learn. Although psychologists have amassed great quantities of empirical data and some impressive theories about learning, much of that knowledge remains buried in technical journals, inaccessible to the professor—at this point a layman—who must busy himself with the technical literature of his own field. There are a few books, which are really not books about college teaching, which summarize some of the significant findings of psychologists who have studied human learning. The books are written by psychologists more as textbooks for students than as books for teachers; nevertheless, some are helpful and deserve mention.

By far the best known and most respected are the works of Ernest Hilgarde, which provide the most comprehensive summaries of various theories about learning. Hilgarde edited the 63rd Yearbook of the National Society for the Study of Education, a volume entitled *Theories of Learning and Instruction* (Chicago: University of Chicago Press, 1964). More recently, he has updated a book, which he co-authored originally with Gordon Bower, entitled *Theories of Learning* (3rd ed.) (New York: Appleton-Century-Crofts, 1966). Also helpful is a book by James Deese and Stewart H. Hulse entitled *The Psychology of Learning* (New York: McGraw-Hill, 1967). A text in the McGraw-Hill Series in Psychology, the Deese and Hulse volume contains helpful chapters on verbal learning, concept learning, and memory as well as basic expositions of reinforcement theory. Three other volumes deserve mention. They are Winfred F. Hill's *Learning: A Survey of Psychological Interpretations* (Scranton, Penna.: Chandler Publishing, 1971), Morris Bigge's *Learning Theories for Teachers* (New York: Harper and Row, 1971), and Sarnoff Mednick's *Learning* (Englewood Cliffs, N.J.: Prentice Hall, 1964). The latter is a volume in Prentice Hall's Foundations of Modern Psychology Series.

The problem with such books is that college teachers usually won't take the time to read them, and if they do, they are often unable to make the necessary transfer and application of theory to their own instructional situation. Alas, college professors become the victims of their profession: They are unable to draw upon and apply the knowledge of another discipline in solving the problems of instruction in their own. The fact that there are books about college teaching and books about learning theory as discrete and distinct categories says something about the way professors compartmentalize thinking about teaching.

## Explications of a Particular Approach to Teaching

Some college teachers have read well into a particular school of psychology and have become disciples of some specific teaching strategy. Some have become "behaviorists" and spell out all that a teacher does in terms of behavioral theory. Others have become dedicated to the use of group methods and view teaching as primarily a group interaction process. Others see teaching as closely allied with facilitating self-actualization and growth and speak of teaching as primarily a matter of establishing authentic human relationships. In recent years a few books have appeared which are explications of a particular approach to teaching.

122

Some particular theory or concept of teaching serves as the thesis of the book, and the argument is established by presenting cases and examples of teaching which demonstrate the theory.

Several recent books address the question of classroom dynamics by exploring concerns and describing techniques which have grown out of the human potential or group dynamics movement. Richard D. Mann's book, *The College Classroom: Conflict, Change and Learning* (New York: John Wiley and Sons, 1970), studies the emotional and interpersonal events that occur in the classroom. Phillip Runkel, Roger Harrison, and Margaret Runkel have described a number of innovative teaching strategies for particular courses, most of which are based on group process theory, in their book *The Changing College Classroom* (San Francisco: Jossey-Bass, 1969). A slightly different type of book is Don M. Flourney and associates' *The New Teachers* (San Francisco: Jossey-Bass, 1972). It contains a series of autobiographical sketches of "new teachers" who use experimental approaches to teaching best described as "open-ended," "student-centered," and "nonauthoritarian." The most recent of such books is Herbert M. Greenberg's *To Educate With Love* (New York: Macmillan, 1974), a sentimental, soft-minded exposition of some principles that grow out of what has come to be called "humanistic psychology." Greenberg wants students to work in groups and to learn how to inquire, something Greenberg feels happens best when professors become authentic persons who really love their students.

Quite different is John Roueche and John Pitman's *A Modest Proposal: Students Can Learn* (San Francisco: Jossey-Bass, 1972). Although the book claims to be addressed to the community-college instructor, it is primarily a solid exposition of what I have called the "systems approach" to instruction and has much in common with the mastery learning theory discussed under "Teaching Strategy 1." A student-centered approach is advocated by Robert Diamond in *Instructional*

*Development for Individualized Learning in Higher Education* (Englewood Cliffs, N.J.: Educational Technology Publications, 1975). Much of the book is concerned with the mechanics of establishing an individualized program, but it is a valuable perspective on several dimensions of one approach to instruction.

Although the books which are explications of a particular strategy or approach to learning are limited by their commitment to a single theory, they are helpful in that they make the effort to bridge the gap between theory and practice. They are self-conscious about methodology and encourage the reader to think deeply about the learning process. One cannot read them without carrying on an internal debate with the authors, and they provide a healthy mixture of theory and practical suggestions. We should have more books like these, and they hold forth promise of effecting change in the attitudes and teaching methodology of those professors who read them.

## Books about Using Media

For some time now college teachers have been aware of the so-called "new media" available as instructional aids. The improvement of instruction has often been linked to greater and more effective use of audio-visual materials, and several books have focused on the use of media in college teaching. In 1968 the American Association for Higher Education and the National Education Association co-sponsored a publication on various new forms of educational technology being employed by colleges and universities across the nation. The book, authored by James Thornton and James Brown, and entitled *New Media and College Teaching* (Washington: National Education Association, 1968), is helpful because it gives specific examples of how media are used at particular institutions.

Sidney Tickton has edited a two-volume study of media entitled *To Improve Learning: An Evaluation of Instructional Technology* (New York: Bowker, 1970). R. Dubin and R. Hedley have summarized the research on instructional uses of television in *The Medium May Be Related to the Message: College Instruction by TV* (Eugene: University of Oregon, 1968). A helpful recent discussion of the new media is the Carnegie Commission study which resulted in *The Fourth Revolution: Instructional Technology in Higher Education* (New York: McGraw-Hill, 1972). *Improving Instructional Productivity in Higher Education* (Englewood Cliffs, N.J.: Educational Technology Publications, 1975), edited by Shelley Harrison and Lawrence Stolurow, is a report of a symposium on technology-based systems for improving productivity in higher education. The book examines various technologies as they relate to three learning environments: grouped, individualized, and personalized.

Although the use of new media can significantly improve instruction, the authors of these volumes are quick to point out that the new media *in themselves* will probably not revolutionize teaching. But the media can serve as a medium (if you will excuse the pun) for stimulating college teachers to be more analytical about the process of instruction with the result that instructional methods will be selected more carefully.

## Summaries of Research Studies on College Teaching

Research on college teaching, however inadequate its design and inconclusive its results, has been undertaken for several decades. Occasionally a scholar will draw together several studies and try to interpret significant trends in the research. One of the oldest of such books is Sidney Pressey's *Research Adventures in University*

*Teaching: Eighteen Investigations Regarding College and University Problems* (Bloomington, Ind.: Public School Publishing Co., 1927). It is interesting to note that research on college teaching has such a long history.

One of the better summaries of research studies is to be found in N. L. Gage's *Handbook of Research on Teaching* (Chicago: Rand McNally, 1963). The most comprehensive summary is to be found in a study by Robert Dubin and Thomas C. Taveggia entitled *The Teaching-Learning Paradox* (Eugene: University of Oregon Press, 1968). A helpful collection of research articles can be found in Richard G. Anderson's *Current Research on Instruction* (Englewood Cliffs, N.J.: Prentice-Hall, 1969).

The research on college teaching has been discussed in detail in the first chapter of this volume. It is important to note here that while there has been little written about the actual teaching-learning process in the college classroom, there have been a significant number of research studies exploring the nature of effective instruction. Once again, doing research on college teaching has been conceived of as a "separate compartment," separate from theorizing about the teaching strategies that might be used in classroom instruction.

## Guidebooks for Evaluating Teaching

Evaluating teaching performance has become increasingly important in recent years. During the "boom" years of the '60s, a college dean was lucky to have anyone to fill his vacancies, and making fine discriminations between "good" and "mediocre" teachers was of little importance. Today the situation is quite different. Administrators and department chairmen are using caution in hiring new personnel and renewing contracts, and in many instances

126

they are called upon to make significant reductions in overall faculty size. Knowing which teachers are the "good" teachers has become increasingly important. Furthermore, students have begun to enter the evaluation process and are demanding a voice in evaluating teacher performance.

Several recent volumes focus on the problem of evaluating faculty performance. One, mentioned earlier, a part of Kenneth Eble's national study, is entitled *The Recognition and Evaluation of Teaching* (Washington: American Association of University Professors and Association of American Colleges, 1970). Another volume, replete with sample forms used for gathering data, is Richard Miller's *Evaluating Faculty Performance* (San Francisco: Jossey-Bass, 1972). Miller's second book, *Developing Programs for Faculty Evaluation* (San Francisco: Jossey-Bass, 1974), focuses on the creation of a total evaluation program within an institution. A fourth volume is R. C. Wilson and M. Hildebrand's *Effective University Teaching and Its Evaluation* (Berkeley, Calif.: Center for Research and Development in Higher Education, 1970). John Centra, in *Two Studies on the Utility of Student Ratings for Instructional Improvement* (Princeton, N.J.: Educational Testing Service, 1972), focuses on the effectiveness of student feedback in modifying college instruction and on a comparison of teachers' self-ratings with student ratings. *Evaluating Learning and Teaching,* edited by C. Robert Pace (San Francisco: Jossey-Bass, 1973), explores the complexity of the evaluation process, emphasizing the necessity of understanding characteristics of students, faculty, courses, teaching, and measures of achievement, before establishing an evaluation program. Peter Seldin, in a book entitled *How Colleges Evaluate Professors* (New York: Blythe-Pennington, 1975), reviews faculty evaluation practices in 410 private liberal arts colleges throughout the country. The study shows that more emphasis is now being placed on what professors are doing on campus rather than off campus. One of the most recent publications on evaluation is *College Professors and Their Impact on Students* (New York: Wiley-Interscience, 1975) by Robert Wilson, Jerry Gaff,

Evelyn Dienst, Lynn Wood, and James Bavry. The multiple authorship and emphasis on methodology make the book difficult to read; it does, however, represent an attempt to draw conclusions from data from 1,000 faculty members at six colleges and universities. The data concern not only teaching practices, but also attitudes and values of the faculty members.

Any solid evaluation of teaching effectiveness should rest, it would seem, upon a fairly sophisticated conceptual understanding of what learning is. As I have discussed in the concluding chapter of this volume, many of the attempts to evaluate college teaching have been superficial. Such "evaluations" of teaching are probably useful in identifying in our midst the very worst teachers, but they are not very helpful in making subtle discriminations based on the teacher's effectiveness in helping students to learn. Until we develop a better understanding of teaching effectiveness, it is unlikely that our evaluation techniques will have much power or usefulness.

## Books on Faculty Development

In the past several years the topic of faculty development has been referred to frequently in the literature on teaching. Faculty development programs, primarily oriented toward teaching improvement, have been implemented in many colleges and universities across the country.

The first volume of the Jossey-Bass series New Directions for Higher Education is entitled *Facilitating Faculty Development* (San Francisco: Jossey-Bass, 1973). The book, edited by Mervin Freedman, includes nine articles by various authors. Topics examined include the changing faculty role, teaching as an art, faculty response to students, the definition of faculty development, and various approaches to faculty development. This volume is valuable since it attempts to explore the various dimensions of the concept of faculty development which includes, but is not limited to, teaching.

A publication by the Group for Human Development in Higher Education, *Faculty Development in a Time of Retrenchment* (New Rochelle, N.Y.: Change Publications, 1974), focuses specifically on teaching development. It describes teaching as a performing art, presents information about the learning process, and comments on the training and evaluation of teachers. The short volume concludes with seven recommendations which are termed "strategies on how to begin revitalizing campus teaching."

A book which refers to specific faculty development programs is *Facilitating Study of College Teaching* by Joseph Leese, Richard Clark, and Robert Kelley (Albany: State University of New York, 1970). This is a summary report of the faculty development program at SUNY (Albany) and describes in detail the activities designed to focus on faculty members' disciplines, objectives, and instructional processes. A similar book is Terry O'Banion's *Teachers for Tomorrow: Staff Development in the Community-Junior College* (Tucson: University of Arizona Press, 1972). Especially helpful in this book is an appendix which describes a wide range of specific pre- and in-service programs for community-junior college faculty.

A recent book by William H. Bergquist and Steven R. Phillips, *A Handbook for Faculty Development* (Washington: The Council for the Advancement of Small Colleges, 1975), focuses on three aspects of development, instructional, organizational, and personal, with a variety of exercises, instruments, and handouts provided for each topic.

# Books about the Profession of Professor

As any professor knows, being a professor involves more than being a college teacher; the multiplicity of roles is sometimes overwhelming. There are several books about the profession as a whole, books that "tell what it is like" to be a college professor. Very often, buried within them, are some observations about college teaching, teaching effectiveness, and the nature of instruction at the college level.

Probably the best known of such books is Robert Bowen's *The New Professors* (New York: Holt, Rinehart and Winston, 1960). It is a collection of chapters written by different college professors and has as its goal the breakdown of stereotypes. It attempts to "show what the profession looks like from the inside." Another notable classic, still well worth reading, is Jacques Barzun's *Teacher in America* (New York: Doubleday and Co., 1955).

Two notable books were published in the 1960s at a time when recruiting scholars to the teaching profession seemed like a necessary thing to do. They are Robert Friedberg's *Careers in College Teaching* (New York: H. Z. Walck, 1965) and Fred Millett's *Professor: Problems and Rewards in College Teaching* (New York: Macmillan, 1961). The latter is one of a series of books on various professions. Kenneth Eble's works listed above under Studies Sponsored by Professional Associations should be mentioned again here. They are *Professors as Teachers* and *Career Development of Effective College Teachers*. A good recent anthology about the profession is Charles Anderson and John Murray's *The Professors: Work and Life Styles Among Academicians* (Cambridge, Mass.: Schenkman, 1971).

Volumes about the profession serve as a reminder that teaching is but one role of the professor. It is still surprising that we have several books about the profession of teaching without much significant discussion of what takes place in the classroom.

## Books on Special Aspects of College Teaching

One would expect that each academic field or discipline would have produced several books on the specialized aspects of teaching that discipline. This is hardly the case; to the contrary, one looks in vain for a single book in some fields. There are, to be sure, numerous books produced by teacher educators directed toward teaching various subjects at the elementary and secondary school levels. But there are very few such specialized books which focus on instruction at the college level.

The following are examples of books about teaching a particular subject: John Gerber's *The College Teaching of English* (New York: Appleton-Century Crofts, 1965), J. Burl Hogins and Gerald Bryant's *A Perceptual Approach to College English: Experiments in Composition* (Riverside, Calif.: Glencoe Press, 1970), *Speaking About English: Papers from the 1965 Summer Session of the Commission on English* (New York: College Entrance Examination Board), Robert Connery's *Teaching Political Science: A Challenge to Higher Education* (Durham, N.C.: Duke University Press, 1965), Claude Buxton's *Improving Undergraduate Instruction in Psychology* (New York: Macmillan, 1952), and Clyde Holbrook's *Religion, A Humanistic Field* (Englewood Cliffs, N.J.: Prentice-Hall, 1963).

One of the more interesting books for those who teach in the humanities is Joseph Axelrod's *The University Teacher as Artist* (San Francisco: Jossey-Bass, 1973).

Axelrod divides teachers into two groups, those who use didactic methods and those who use evocative methods. The latter are the true artists and can be divided into four prototypes: the principles and facts type, the instructor-centered type, the student-as-mind type, and the student-as-person type. The more interesting aspect of Axelrod's work is the use he makes of illustrations, transcripts of actual class settings which enable the reader to look into the classroom and watch evocative teacher-artists teach.

Among the new or specialized books on teaching in a particular setting are those addressed to teachers in community colleges. Roger Harrison has produced a helpful monograph for the American Association of Junior Colleges entitled *Teaching in a Junior College: A Brief Professional Orientation* (Washington: American Association of Junior Colleges, 1968). Two other books that focus on community-college teaching are Win Kelley and Leslie Wilbur's *Teaching in the Community-Junior College* (New York: Appleton-Century Crofts, 1970) and Arthur Cohen and Florence Brawer's *Confronting Identity: The Community College Instructor* (Englewood Cliffs, N.J.: Prentice-Hall, 1972).

In addition there are occasional books on teaching in a specialized setting such as H. M. LaFauci and P. Richter's *Team Teaching at the College Level* (Elmsford, N.Y.: Pergamon Press, 1970) and Perry Le Fevre's *The Christian Teacher* (New York: Abingdon Press, 1958). Such books necessarily focus more on the special characteristics of the setting than on the fundamental nature of the teaching process.

There is a need for more such specialized works, particularly works written by specialists in a discipline. Hopefully such authors will focus on the process of instruction as well as its content and will themselves have a good grasp of various teaching strategies.

## The Literature on College Teaching: Some Conclusions

Ironically, most of the books about college teaching are not about college teaching at all. They are about almost everything but college teaching. They discuss current issues in higher education, the history of higher education, and the aims of education. They exhort their readers to better teaching. They describe in detail the context in which teaching is carried on, how teachers are educated, and how good teaching is rewarded or neglected. They tell what it is like to be a college teacher, how to evaluate college teaching, and what research on teaching has been done. But only rarely, if at all, is there any discussion of *the actual teaching-learning process itself*. It is as if there is a systematic avoidance of the subject, as with a cultural taboo. Writers on the subject venture to the very edge of talking about something significant, but then fail to take the plunge. Or if they do, they speak in platitudes and with an awesome vagueness. Their exhortations are like the echoing screams coming from someone plunging into an abyss—screams followed by silence. Why is it that we find so little direct discussion of teaching strategies for the college classroom?

First of all, as I have noted in the first chapter of this volume, the process of teaching has been governed by conventions; and conventions are, by their very nature, ways of proceeding which are accepted and not questioned. To the extent that college teachers have thought about what they are doing, their critical insights have been cast in philosophical categories. College teachers have been particularly adept at defending conventional approaches to instruction by hiding behind a false modesty with regard to knowledge about teaching. Anyone who would claim to "know" something about college teaching must surely be pretentious. But all of that is changing. New knowledge about how people learn is coming from various disciplines, primarily from psychology and communications theory. While there is no agreement upon any single theory of learning, there is, nevertheless, a great deal of knowledge today about how people learn. Part of the reason why so little has been written about the process of college teaching is that what is known has been discovered recently, and what we know has had to make headway against powerful, long-standing conventions.

Second, the improvement of college instruction involves a host of complex problems not likely to be solved by the insights of a single discipline. The compartmentalization of knowledge into academic disciplines has proven to be a serious drawback to the solution of many contemporary social problems. Some universities have developed structures for solving social problems which cut across disciplines, e.g., urban studies and environmental studies programs. The improvement of college teaching is that kind of problem; its solution requires integration and cross-disciplinary understandings rather than a com- partmentalized approach. But there are books on college teaching which display no working knowledge of learning theory, and there are books on learning theory with no immediately apparent relevance for college teaching. There are separate books on research studies, on evaluation of teaching, and on the new media. The studies are very much compartmentalized, and as such are able to contribute only in limited ways to the improvement of teaching. The apparent lack of depth in much of the literature about college teaching is a result of academic com- partmentalization, a failure to bring to the problem analyses sufficiently complex to be of value.

Third, the improvement of college teaching rests heavily on the application of theory in practice. Academicians, for many justifiable reasons, are reluctant to spend much time demonstrating to others how to apply what is known. The academic world places a premium on theoretical knowledge and leaves to the technician the task of applying what is known in the solution of a specific problem. Psychologists, for example, are reluctant to spend much time demonstrating the myriad applications of a particular learning theory. They are eager to move on to the next theoretical problem suggested by their research. Unfortunately, higher education has few technicians who are willing to spend time applying what is known about teaching and learning to the task of college teaching. The literature on college teaching reveals that there are few good technicians, in this sense of the word, who are able to translate—even popularize—what is known about learning into forms that are applicable to the specific tasks of teachers.

Fourth, the academic reward system discourages outstanding scholars from publishing books about instruction in their discipline. The imperative to publish is a specific command; not "just anything" will do. Given the choice between doing a definitive study of Robert Frost and a handbook on teaching American poetry, the young scholar will obviously choose the more respected (more scholarly?) work on Frost. The young biologist will undertake some replication of a fruit-fly experiment with a new twist, rather than think deeply about the process of laboratory instruction. The paucity of books on teaching some aspect of a particular field is a vacuous testimony to the fact that academia does not reward or respect reflection on the process of teaching by its more outstanding scholars.

Students, society at large, and more recently professors themselves have criticized higher education for its compartmentalization of inquiry into disciplines and its reluctance to suggest concrete applications for what is known. Ironically, college teachers have become the victims of the inadequacies of a system they have long perpetuated. As long as the problem was "out there" somewhere in society, the charges of "overspecialization" and "irrelevance" could be brushed aside. But now the charges once denied have returned to haunt those who are under great pressure, and will be increasingly, to improve their teaching. The improvement of instruction will depend on the ability of professors to solve a problem which defies compartmentalization and calls out for the application of theory in practice.

What is needed? There are many gaps in the literature. We do not need more general books on college teaching. We do not need books that discuss "methods" or summarize endless numbers of research studies using obviously faulty designs. We don't need any more books that tell what it is "really like" to be a college teacher. What we do need are some good multivariate design research studies. We need books that are designed to bridge the gap between theory and practice, that translate technical knowledge into guidelines that will improve teaching. We need penetrating discussions of the nature of the teaching-learning process in a college classroom. We need in almost every discipline books which speak to the specialized problems of instruction in a particular subject. We need books which synthesize what is known about teaching and learning and what is known about faculty evaluation, new media, and research. We need books which are explications of a particular theory of instruction and which provide concrete examples of how to teach a particular subject in a particular way. In short, we need more books on college teaching, but they must be different from most of those published in the past.

This present volume takes its place in a rather extensive literature about college teaching. Like other books on college teaching, it serves limited purposes and has its own modest goals. But whatever its limitation, it is hoped that those who read it will say, "This is one book on college teaching that provides teaching strategies that can be used in the college classroom."